HAROLD
BRIGHOUSE

HOBSON'S
CHOICE

Notes and questions by Tim Bezant

Heinemann Educational Publishers
Halley Court, Jordan Hill, Oxford OX2 8EJ
a division of Reed Educational & Professional Publishing Ltd
OXFORD   MELBOURNE   AUCKLAND
JOHANNESBURG   BLANTYRE   GABORONE
IBADAN   PORTSMOUTH (NH) USA   CHICAGO

First published by Samuel French Ltd in 1956
First published in Heinemann's *Hereford Plays* series 1964
First published in the *Heinemann Plays* series 1992
05 04 03 02 01
18 17 16 15

A catalogue record for this book is available from the British Library on request.
ISBN 0 435 23280 0

Cover design by Keith Pointing
Designed by Jeffrey White Creative Associates
Typeset by Taurus Graphics
Printed by Clays Ltd, St Ives plc

CONTENTS

PREFACE

In this edition of *Hobson's Choice*, you will find notes, questions and activities to help in studying the play in class, particularly at GCSE level.

The introduction provides background information on the author, the writing of the play, the circumstances of its first production and its place in English theatrical tradition and development.

The activities at the end of the book range from straightforward *Keeping Track* questions which can be tackled at the end of each act to focus close attention on what is happening in the play, through more detailed work on characters and themes in *Explorations*, to more advanced discussion questions under *Criticism*.

There is also a bibliography with details of other books about Harold Brighouse's work. Right at the end of the book is a glossary, arranged by acts, for easy reference.

If you are already using the Hereford edition of *Hobson's Choice*, you will find that the page numbering in the actual playscript is the same, so allowing the two editions to be easily used side by side.

INTRODUCTION

Harold Brighouse

Harold Brighouse was born on 26 July 1882 in Eccles, near Salford, Lancashire. His father, John Brighouse, worked for the Manchester cotton business of Holdsworth and Gibb, was a magistrate and treasurer of the Eccles Liberal Association: according to his son, he was 'addicted to work'. Before her marriage, his mother had been a headmistress. His parents' marriage in 1881 broke the conventions of the time, for John Brighouse had previously been married to his second wife's sister: as a result, until the law was later changed, Harold and his sister Hilda were technically illegitimate. To Brighouse, however, his parents' marriage 'asserted independence of mind; and it was an affirmation of love'.

Brighouse was, therefore, brought up happily in a secure middle-class family: 'we must have seemed a prosperous assembly', he wrote in his autobiography. At times, however, this security was endangered by the erratic performance of Holdsworth and Gibb, which John Brighouse struggled to keep balanced, and by the frequent and occasionally large loans he made to his brothers and relatives. Rather, this was a closely accounted, almost frugal prosperity, from which Brighouse's mother hoped her son would progress to emulate her brother Edwin, a classics genius who had died young. She taught Harold at home, enabling him to win a scholarship to Manchester Grammar School. Brighouse was, in his own words, 'unteachable', and while school provided him with an education his mother 'was to be disappointed' in her high ambitions for him. Rather than follow a possibly unproductive career at university, and impressed by his father's work in the cotton business, Brighouse left school at seventeen to learn the cotton trade in a shipping merchant's warehouse.

'Where, then, did the theatre come in?', he asks himself in his autobiography. 'Effectively, nowhere.' In fact, working in central Manchester, Brighouse was surrounded by theatres and it was a summer season of Shakespeare plays at the Theatre Royal in 1900 that awakened his interest in drama. When he moved to London on business in 1902 his playgoing became voracious, and he became a regular attender at the first nights of new plays: 'It was a first-nighter's point of honour to miss no first performance. The gallery cost a shilling. Quantity could be coped with.' It was during this time that Brighouse saw the plays in the Court Theatre seasons run by Harley Granville-Barker and J E Vedrenne (see below). This period was seen as also his 'rich, random, unpremeditated first apprenticeship to playwriting'.

By now Brighouse was engaged to a fellow theatre-lover. He returned to Manchester to be married but maintained weekly visits to London, combining his cotton business with his pleasure in theatre. During one of these visits, as he describes it, 'I saw the first performance of, as it happened, an outrageously bad play' and suddenly he realised that in all probability he could write a better play himself. His first play was, following the fashion, a five-act romantic drama which he sent to the leading actor-manager J Forbes-Robertson. While he rejected it, Forbes-Robertson advised Brighouse to 'Try one-acters first - to write of the life you know.' Following this advice, Brighouse wrote his first one-act play, *Lonesome-like*, in 1909. While it was not performed until 1911, it set him firmly on the path to becoming a full-time writer.

At about this time, in 1907, the new Gaiety Theatre had been opened in Manchester, with a commitment to producing new plays by local writers (see below). This further fuelled Brighouse's ambition: 'I had been indolent: now I worked.' While still working full-time for his employer as a salesman, he now wrote plays in both the evenings and at weekends. One of these, a one-act play entitled *The Doorway*, was produced at the Gaiety Theatre in 1909. His first full-length play to be performed, *Dealing in Futures*, about workers in a chemical factory poisoned by the dyes with which they work, was produced in Glasgow in 1910, followed by *Lonesome-like* in 1911, which, as a 'curtain-raiser', played before the main play of the evening, ran for 3000 performances.

The success of these plays confirmed Brighouse in his new vocation, and while he maintained his links with the cotton trade until after the First World War, writing was now his true career. *The Game*, about a brilliant young footballer, followed in 1913; *The Northerners*, set in the Lancashire cotton industry of the 1820s, and *Garside's Career*, about the corruption of a young Member of Parliament, were both produced in 1914. At the outbreak of war in 1914, Brighouse was in France working on a music-drama, and it was after his enforced return to England that he wrote *Hobson's Choice* (see below).

The popularity of Brighouse's plays with both theatres and their audiences assured him of success for as long as he cared to write. Subsequent plays included *Zack* (1920), *The Sort-of Prince* (1929) and *Coincidence* (1930). Further security was afforded by the legacy he inherited on his father's death in 1917. He was able to settle permanently in London, and when he chose to give up writing in 1930 his output totalled fifteen full-length and fifty one-act plays. In addition, he also wrote eight novels, including an adaptation of *Hobson's Choice*, as well as critical articles for the *Manchester Guardian* newspaper. He was now able to live off the income from the royalties of his work. His last major piece, published in 1953 (five years before his death in 1958), was his autobiography, *What I Have Had*, on the cover of which he was identified as the author of 'the famous play *Hobson's Choice*'.

It is by this play that Brighouse is now best remembered; its quality was confirmed when it was selected for the National Theatre's repertoire in 1964. A further West End production was presented in 1982, and it was extensively toured in 1989. Further productions continue to be mounted and the film, made in 1954 with Charles Laughton and John Mills, is frequently televised. Its deserved popularity means that, despite all his other work, Brighouse is largely thought of, as he admitted himself, as a 'one-play man'.

The Theatrical Context: The Repertory Movement.

Brighouse is often referred to as a member of the 'Manchester school' of dramatists, whose members also included Stanley Houghton (*Hindle Wakes*, 1911) and Allan Monkhouse. The opening of the new repertory theatre at the Gaiety Theatre in Manchester provided Brighouse, amongst others, with a focus for his playwriting as well as a context for both the style and content of his plays. However, the developments in Manchester were only part of a nationwide trend in the British theatre which had its origins at the end of the nineteenth century.

Dissatisfaction with the poor quality and unchanging commercial content of London's influential West End theatre had led in 1891 to the foundation of the Independent Theatre Society. Its aim was to promote new plays for their own sakes with no consideration for their possible popular appeal. It was this society that first performed many of the now famous and influential plays of the Norwegian Henrik Ibsen and George Bernard Shaw. In doing so, it created an interest in, and a demand for, serious new plays. Its place was taken in 1899 by the Stage Society, an early member of which was Harley Granville-Barker, an actor with experience of various touring companies as well as the West End. Again, the aim of the Society was to restore life to the English theatre by encouraging the writing and performance of new plays. To bring these new plays to a wider audience Granville-Barker hired the Court Theatre in Sloane Square, London, in 1904 for the first in a series of seasons of plays which would start a revolution in British theatre.

It was these seasons of plays at the Court Theatre which Brighouse saw during his time in London and which would influence him in future. These seasons staked their success upon the new plays and the acting alone: the productions were simple and unpretentious but well-rehearsed, allowing the plays to speak for themselves to the audience. Each play was allowed only a short initial run of performances, but was thereafter held in the repertory of the company. As far as possible, the same company of actors was employed throughout the season; there were no stars, as the company itself was to be stronger than any individual member.

At the time, these were entirely revolutionary ideas in the London theatre, which relied heavily upon expensive productions of lightweight plays that were vehicles for popular stars. These plays were run for as long as possible, eventually becoming stale and dead. The intention at the Court Theatre was to keep both the repertoire of plays and the company of actors fresh and the audience interested. Playwrights produced at the Court Theatre between 1904 and 1907 included Shaw, Ibsen, W B Yeats and John Galsworthy, as well as Granville-Barker himself. Despite only just paying his way at the Court Theatre, Granville-Barker hired the Savoy Theatre in the heart of the West End for the 1907-8 season, only to fail in the face of small audiences and large debts.

Despite this, however, the Court Theatre seasons were to be the inspiration for the new repertory theatre companies that were to be founded in several of Britain's major cities in the years that followed.

The first of these was the Gaiety Theatre, established in Manchester in 1907 by Miss Annie Horniman. The heiress to the Horniman's tea fortune, Miss Horniman had already helped to set up the Abbey Theatre in Dublin for the Irish National Theatre Society. After disagreements with the company, which resented its reliance upon an Englishwoman, she sought a new outlet for her enthusiasm in mainland Britain. In collaboration with the former director of the Abbey Theatre, Ben Iden Payne, and not wishing to compete with the Court Company in London, Miss Horniman chose Manchester for her experiment. It was already a cultural centre, supporting its own symphony orchestra, and in addition had already had its own Independent Theatre Society in the 1890s. After a brief but not particularly successful season of plays in the ballroom of the Midland Hotel (rechristened the Midland Theatre), Miss Horniman purchased the Comedy Theatre, renamed it the Gaiety Theatre, and put Iden Payne in charge of its artistic direction.

From the start, the aims of the Gaiety Theatre reflected those of the Court Theatre. Plays were to be presented by a recognisable, constant company, and would be played on short runs and held in repertoire. The presentation of new plays, with the emphasis on local writers, was to be a high priority and, as Payne writes in his autobiography, 'Enough Lancashire playwrights responded and had their plays performed at the Gaiety' that they came to be frequently referred to as the Manchester school.' As has already been noted, Brighouse was one of these writers, and the Gaiety provided him with a necessary focus for his writing at the start of his career. The Gaiety was the first true repertory theatre in Britain, and after an indifferent response to its first full season in Manchester, its future was assured after a successful visit to London. The company survived until 1921, staging over 200 plays, of which over 100 were new plays. While the company could not survive the after-effects of the First World War, the effect of the repertory movement which it had led had changed the face of British Theatre. It was in this context of theatrical change that Brighouse wrote *Hobson's Choice* in 1915.

Hobson's Choice

The phrase 'Hobson's choice' is proverbial; to have Hobson's choice is to have no choice at all. Its origin lies in the practice of the seventeenth-century Cambridgeshire horse trader Hobson, whose customers in theory had a free choice but in practice always ended up with the horse nearest the stable door, which was Hobson's choice.

Its origin as the title of a play is told by Ben Iden Payne in his autobiography. After the performance of a play he had directed at the Gaiety Theatre, Brighouse and his fellow writer Stanley Houghton were sharing a drink with Iden Payne in the bar of the Midland Hotel: they asked him why a particular actor, who had given a bad performance, had been chosen for the part:

'My retort was that it had been Hobson's choice; there was no-one else available who would have been any better. . . No sooner had I said this than it occurred to me that the phrase would make a good title for a play. I said so and Houghton and Brighouse agreed. A friendly argument arose as to which of them should be the author of the hypothetical 'Hobson's Choice'. I suggested that they toss a coin. This they did and Brighouse won.'

As Houghton was not to die until 1913, and the play was not written until 1914-15, it is clear that the gestation period for the play in Brighouse's imagination was a long one.

As noted above, Brighouse was working in France at the declaration of war in 1914. As a foreign national in a nation that conscripted its young men into its army, he was forced to leave immediately. He made his way to the coast in a bus full of men, all of whom, including the driver, were on their way to enlist; the only three women on board hardly ceased crying throughout the journey: 'here in the raw was shown to me what war meant to the common men and women of a conscript nation. That bus collaborated with me in writing *Hobson's Choice*.' Clearly this journey, and the relatively recent death of his friend Houghton, moved Brighouse deeply. As he wrote in his autobiography:

'Emotional experience is written off by an author in a form which may bear no resemblance to the originating disturbance. . . I was a writer with an emotional load to get rid of, and at a sharp tangent to the bus to Havre I recollected Salford, where in Cross Lane my father was born, and I wrote *Hobson's Choice*.'

The play was written rapidly; 'too rapidly till a useful influenza compelled a reflective pause.' It seems that in the enforced break Brighouse changed the course of the final act and set the play back in time from 1914-15 to 1880, which he later considered added to the play's depth and helped to save it from an early oblivion.

In an atmosphere of enforced jollity designed to divert the troops at home on leave from their experiences at war, London producers refused the play in 1915, despite the author's past pedigree. Instead, he sent the play to his friend Iden Payne, now working in New York, who, impressed with the play, persuaded his employers in the Schubert organisation to produce it. After only a week's tour, and after uncertainty over whether the play would open at all in New York City, *Hobson's Choice* finally opened there at the Comedy Theatre. It was well received by both audiences and theatre critics alike, whose reviews read like 'an actor's dream', and it went on to run for several months.

This success paved the way for the London presentation of the play at the Apollo Theatre in 1916. It was prepared in a fortnight and opened on 22 June to be greeted in the press as a 'real success . . . *Hobson's Choice* will rank among the English plays of the day'. In working out his own emotional upset through his Lancashire comedy, Brighouse touched a nerve in the theatre-going public; so much so that it was to run for 246 performances at the Apollo and Prince of Wales theatres.

In Performance

The initial reviews of the play clearly identified those qualities which made it such a success: 'Mr Brighouse has portrayed these people just as he knows and sees them, and the result is true comedy – highly diverting and rich in human nature.' The characters, rather than any action or event, are the focus of the play, which shows how Maggie Hobson, the stronger daughter of a strong boot-selling father, is able to break away from his overbearing household through her marriage to Willie Mossop, her father's principal bootmaker, while also providing the means for her sisters to marry the men of their choice – and all against their father's wishes. The final act shows the consequences of the action of the first three acts, and provides the final blow for Hobson as, sick in both body and business, Willie and Maggie, newly successful, return to save Hobson from himself, on their own terms.

A successful production of the play would show how the action arises naturally from the strong (and in the case of Willie Mossop, weak) characters. Hobson's single-mindedness, shown in the way he attempts to live his life, run his house and rule his daughters, is also seen in each of his daughters. It is seen in Maggie's dominance and grooming of Willie, in her devious acquisition of her sister's dowries and, not least, in her finally, at the age of 30, standing up to her father. In their lesser, possibly more selfish ways, Alice and Vickey have also inherited this characteristic. What sets Maggie apart from the rest of her family is that she uses this quality, not only for her own benefit, but also for the benefit of others; not least, though he is initially unconvinced, Willie Mossop.

The story of the play is also the story of the transformation of Willie. Maggie has the 'very keen eye' required in the stage direction on page 9 to detect Willie's potential; not only that, she has the determination and ability to make him into the man of whom she wants to be proud. Yet it is clearly shown in Acts 1-3 that the man Willie will become in Act 4 is already latent within him. All Maggie does in the intervening year is to bring it out; yet without her, he would have been a humble boot-maker all his life. The transformation in his character takes place offstage; a successful presentation of the character would need to make Willie's potential equally clear to the audience when appropriate, so that the character presented in the final act would not come as an unbelievable surprise.

If the play presents the rise of Maggie and Willie, it also presents the fall of Henry Horatio Hobson. The seeds of his downfall are clearly signalled to the audience in the first act. He neglects his business, and relies on his daughters' rapidly diminishing goodwill to run both his shop and his household. At the same time, he insists on being recognised as the head of both while in fact he contributes little to either. Instead, his energies are devoted to passing his time with his drinking friends at the Moonraker's public house. His overbearing sense of his own self-importance is revealed in his attitudes to his children and the others around him and in his ostentatious vocabulary and manner of speaking. The comedy in the character arises from the contrast in how he sees himself and how other people see him (according to their own circumstances), and from his attempts to impose his own opinion and sense of himself upon them. A successful presentation of the play should never present Hobson as totally unsympathetic, as the comedy would otherwise evaporate.

While the other characters in the play all have a function to perform, none are as vivid as the central five. Jim Heeler is Hobson's bosom friend and confidant; Tubby is used later in the play to show the deterioration in Hobson's business. Albert Prosser and Fred Beenstock are Alice and Vickey's suitors and, through careful plotting, are also a lawyer and trader respectively, each of whom have a part to play in Maggie's plotting against her father. Ada Figgins's brief appearance shows the contrast that Maggie represents to Willie and also allows Brighouse to entertain the audience by overturning the convention in drama of two men fighting over a woman by showing Maggie and Ada battling for Willie. Mrs Hepworth is the only real customer seen in the play yet her real function is to bring about our introduction to Willie and, later, to finance Willie and Maggie's business. Finally, Dr MacFarlane, perhaps a stereotype, diagnoses Hobson's final weakness and prescribes the necessary cure, thus effectively setting up the final confrontation between Maggie and Willie, and Hobson. A successful production would, of course, integrate these characters fully into the action, so that the audience was unaware of their dramatic functions.

The language of the play and the manner in which the characters express themselves are particularly important to the tone of the play; it is, after all, a 'Lancashire comedy' and it was this feature which contributed in no small measure to its original success. The examples of the Lancashire dialect (that is, those aspects of vocabulary and expression particular to Salford at that time) are intrinsic to both the characters and the situations.

Particular characters are distinguished through the language that they use: the most obvious example is Hobson himself, whose choice of vocabulary and sentence structures has already been noted. The sentence structures embody the conversational rhythms of the dialect in a realistic, naturalistic manner which lends credibility to the characters who speak them: a vivid example is Willie's final defiant speech at the end of Act 1. While in performance the sharpness of the dialogue would be a source of humour in itself, it forms a constituent part of the greater comedy arising from the interaction of the characters.

Finally, in performance three settings would be required: Hobson's shop, Willie Mossop's shop in the cellar of 39A Oldfield Road, and the living-room of Hobson's shop. In keeping with the tone of the play, the stage directions for the settings at the starts of each act are detailed, realistic and precise: Brighouse uses them to convey to the audience vital detail about the characters who inhabit these surroundings. Both the settings and the costumes used in a faithful production of the play would need to be realistic to the period, 1880-1.

Reading the Play

All plays are written to be performed or, at the very least, read aloud. This is doubly true of *Hobson's Choice*: only in reading the play aloud will the naturalistic, conversational nature of the play become fully clear. Through hearing the characters speak, a fuller understanding of their attitudes and opinions, both of themselves and of others, will be formed. Arising from this, it will be possible to develop a sense of how the characters would show their opinions and reactions in other, physical ways. Only through an effective reading of the play can an understanding of the various characters' changes and interactions begin to be developed.

While the play is constructed from four acts, various 'scenes' within the acts are easily identifiable: they are usually marked by the entrance or exit of a particular character. This obviously lends particular parts of the play to detailed study or to reading and rehearsing in small groups. A useful approach is to read sections aloud first of all to understand the action and the relationships; then explore and experiment with the text to discover more depth and understanding of the characters and their changing relationships.

Following the play text you will find a *Glossary* designed to explain particular references and examples of dialect. Two series of questions are entitled *Keeping Track* and *Explorations*. *Keeping Track* is intended to help your understanding of the action and characters as the play develops and can be used while reading the play for the first time. *Explorations* are more detailed and demanding questions organised according to character, themes, performance and criticism. The questions in this section may lead to coursework assignments or examination practice. All the questions are designed to stimulate knowledge, understanding and, hopefully, enjoyment of the play.

Tim Bezant

List of Characters and Acts

Characters

Alice Hobson
Maggie Hobson
Vickey Hobson
Albert Prosser
Henry Horatio Hobson
Mrs Hepworth
Timothy Wadlow (Tubby)
William Mossop
Jim Heeler
Ada Figgins
Fred Beenstock
Dr Macfarlane

The scene of the play is in Salford, Lancashire, and the period is 1880.

Hobson's Choice was originally produced in America. The first London production took place on 22 June 1916 at the Apollo Theatre, with the following cast:

Henry Horatio Hobson	Norman McKinnel
Maggie Hobson	Edyth Goodall
William Mossop	Joe Nightingale
Alice Hobson	Lydia Bilbrooke
Vickey Hobson	Hilda Davies
Albert Prosser	Reginald Fry
Fred Beenstock	Jefferson Gore
Mrs Hepworth	Dora Gregory
Timothy Wadlow	Sydney Paxton
Jim Heeler	J. Cooke Beresford
Ada Figgins	Mary Byron
Dr Macfarlane	J. Fisher White

The Play produced by Norman Mckinnel

The play has had many notable productions since its first production in 1916, and it was included in the National Theatre repertory on 7 January 1964, with the following cast:

Henry Horatio Hobson	Michael Redgrave
Maggie Hobson	Joan Plowright
William Mossop	Frank Finlay
Alice Hobson	Mary Miller
Vickey Hobson	Jeanne Hepple
Albert prosser	Terence Knapp
Fred beenstock	Raymond Clarke
Mrs Hepworth	Enid Lorimer
Timothy wadlow	Reginald Green
Jim Heeler	Henry Lomax
Ada figgins	Jean Rogers
Dr macfarlane	Anthony Nichols

Scenery and costumes by Motley
The Play directed by John Dexter

ACT ONE

(handwritten annotations) prosperas - but catering for poorer people (factories) doing well - (Worker-Class) Probably not in a posh area The Shope is dull, dark, dreary

The scene represents the interior of Hobson's Boot Shop in Chapel Street, Salford. The shop windows and entrance from street occupy the left side. Facing the audience is the counter, with exhibits of boots and slippers, behind which the wall is filled with racks containing boot boxes. Cane chairs in front of counter. There is a desk down left with a chair. A door right leads up to the house. In the centre of the stage is a trap leading to the cellar where work is done. There are no elaborate fittings. Gas brackets in the windows and walls. The business is prosperous, but to prosper in Salford in 1880 you did not require the elaborate accessories of a later day. A very important customer goes for fitting into Hobson's sitting-room. The rank and file use the cane chairs in the shop, which is dingy but business-like. The windows exhibit little stock, and amongst what there is clogs figure prominently. Through the windows comes the bright light of noon.

Sitting behind the counter are Hobson's two younger daughters, ALICE, *who is twenty-three, and* VICTORIA, *who is twenty-one, and very pretty.* ALICE *is knitting and* VICTORIA *is reading. They are in black, with neat black aprons. The door opens, and* MAGGIE *enters. She is Hobson's eldest daughter, thirty.*

ALICE	Oh, it's you. I hoped it was father going out.
MAGGIE	It isn't. (*She crosses and takes her place at desk.*)
ALICE	He *is* late this morning.
MAGGIE	He got up late. (*She busies herself with an account book.*)
VICKEY	(*reading*): Has he had breakfast yet, Maggie?
MAGGIE	Breakfast! With a Masons' meeting last night?

VICKEY   He'll need reviving.

ALICE   Then I wish he'd go and do it.

VICKEY   Are you expecting anyone, Alice?

ALICE   Yes, I am, and you know I am, and I'll thank you both to go when he comes.

VICKEY   Well, I'll oblige you, Alice, if father's gone out first, only you know I can't leave the counter till he goes.

ALBERT PROSSER *enters from the street. He is twenty-six, nicely dressed, as the son of an established solicitor would be. He crosses to counter and raises his hat to Alice.*

ALBERT   Good morning, Miss Alice.

ALICE   Good morning, Mr Prosser. (*She leans across counter.*) Father's not gone out yet. He's late.

ALBERT   Oh! (*He turns to go, and is half-way to the door, when* MAGGIE *rises.*)

MAGGIE   (*rising*): What can we do for you, Mr Prosser?

ALBERT   (*stopping*): Well, I can't say that I came in to buy anything, Miss Hobson.

MAGGIE   This is a shop, you know. We're not here to let people go out without buying.

ALBERT   Well, I'll just have a pair of bootlaces, please.

MAGGIE   What size do you take in boots?   *Albert came to see Alice*

ALBERT   Eights. I've got small feet. (*He simpers, then perceives that Maggie is by no means smiling.*) Does that matter to the laces?

MAGGIE   (*putting mat in front of armchair*): It matters to the boots. (*She pushes him slightly.*) Sit down, Mr Prosser.

ALBERT   (*sitting*): Yes, but –

MAGGIE *is on her knees and takes off his boot.*

MAGGIE   It's time you had a new pair. These uppers are disgraceful for a professional man to wear. Number eights from the third rack, Vickey, please.

ALICE   Mr Prosser didn't come in to buy boots, Maggie.

VICKEY *comes down to Maggie with box, which she opens.*

MAGGIE   I wonder what does bring him in here so often?

ALBERT	I'm terrible hard on bootlaces, Miss Hobson.
	MAGGIE *puts a new boot on him and laces it.*
MAGGIE	Do you get through a pair a day? You must be strong.
ALBERT	I keep a little stock of them. It's as well to be prepared for accidents.
MAGGIE	And now you'll have boots to go with the laces, Mr Prosser. How does that feel?
ALBERT	Very comfortable.
MAGGIE	Try it standing up.
ALBERT	(*trying and walking a few steps*): Yes, that fits all right.
MAGGIE	I'll put the other on.
ALBERT	Oh no, I really don't want to buy them.
MAGGIE	(*pushing him*): Sit down, Mr Prosser. You can't go through the streets in odd boots.
ALBERT	What's the price of these?
MAGGIE	A pound.
ALBERT	A pound! I say –
MAGGIE	They're good boots, and you don't need to buy a pair of laces today, because we give them in as discount. Braid laces, that is. Of course, if you want leather ones, you being so strong in the arm and breaking so many pairs, you can have them, only it's tuppence more.
ALBERT	These – these will do.
MAGGIE	Very well, you'd better have the old pair mended and I'll send them home to you with the bill. (*She has laced the second boot, rises, and moves towards desk, throwing the boot box at* VICKEY, *who gives a little scream at the interruption of her reading.* ALBERT *gasps*).
ALBERT	Well, if anyone had told me I was coming in here to spend a pound I'd have called him crazy.
MAGGIE	It's not wasted. Those boots will last. Good morning, Mr Prosser. (*She holds door open.*)
ALBERT	Good morning. (*He looks blankly at Alice and goes out*).
ALICE	Maggie, we know you're a pushing sales-woman, but–

MAGGIE (*returning to counter she picks up old boots and puts them on rack*): It'll teach him to keep out of here a bit. He's too much time on his hands.

ALICE You know why he comes.

MAGGIE I know it's time he paid a rent for coming. A pair of laces a day's not half enough. Coming here to make sheep's eyes at you. I'm sick of the sight of him. *refers to Albert*

ALICE It's all very well for an old maid like you to talk, but if father won't have us go courting, where else can Albert meet me except here when father's out?

MAGGIE If he wants to marry you why doesn't he do it?

ALICE Courting must come first.

MAGGIE It needn't. (*She picks up a slipper.*) See that slipper with a fancy buckle on to make it pretty? Courting's like that, my lass. All glitter and no use to nobody. (*She replaces slipper and sits at her desk.*)

HOBSON *enters from the house. He is fifty–five, successful, coarse, florid, and a parent of the period. His hat is on. It is one of these felt hats which are half-way to tall hats in shape. He has a heavy gold chain and masonic emblems on it. His clothes are bought to wear.*

HOBSON Maggie, I'm just going out for a quarter of an hour.

MAGGIE Yes, father. Don't be late for dinner. There's liver.

HOBSON It's an hour off dinner-time. (*Going.*)

MAGGIE So that, if you stay more than an hour in the Moonraker's Inn, you'll be late for it.

HOBSON 'Moonraker's'? Who said – ?(*Turning*)

VICKEY If your dinner's ruined, it'll be your own fault.

HOBSON Well, I'll be eternally –

ALICE Don't swear, father.

HOBSON (*putting hat on counter*): No. I'll sit down instead. (*He takes a chair, straddling across it and facing them with his elbows on its back.*) Listen to me, you three. I've come to conclusions about you. And I won't have it. Do you hear that? Interfering with my goings out and comings in. The idea! I've a mind to take measures with the lot of you.

MAGGIE I expect Mr Heeler's waiting for you in 'Moonraker's', father.

HOBSON He can go on waiting. At present, I'm addressing a few remarks to the rebellious females of this house, and what I say will be listened to and heeded. I've noticed it coming on ever since your mother died. There's been a gradual increase of uppishness towards me. *[handwritten annotations: "laughter Down"]*

VICKEY Father, you'd have more time to talk after we've closed tonight. (*She is anxious to resume her reading.*)

HOBSON I'm talking now, and you're listening. Providence has decreed that you should lack a mother's hand at the time when single girls grow bumptious and must have somebody to rule. But I'll tell you this, you'll none rule me.

VICKEY I'm sure I'm not bumptious, father.

HOBSON Yes, you are. You're pretty, but you're bumptious, and I hate bumptiousness like I hate a lawyer. *[handwritten annotations: "embarrassment later in play legal trap"]*

ALICE If we take trouble to feed you it's not bumptious to ask you not to be late for your food.

VICKEY Give and take, father.

HOBSON I give and you take, and it's going to end.

MAGGIE How much a week do you give us?

HOBSON That's neither here nor there. (*Rises and moves to doors.*) At moment I'm on uppishness, and I'm warning you your conduct towards your parent's got to change. (*Turns to the counter.*) But that's not all. That's private conduct, and now I pass to broader aspects and I speak of public conduct. I've looked upon my household as they go about the streets, and I've been disgusted. The fair name and fame of Hobson have been outraged by members of Hobson's family, and uppishness has done it.

VICKEY I don't know what you're talking about.

HOBSON Vickey, you're pretty, but you can lie like a gasmeter. Who had new dresses on last week?

ALICE   I suppose you mean Vickey and me?

HOBSON   I do.

VICKEY   We shall dress as we like, father, and you can save your breath.

HOBSON   I'm not stopping in from my business appointment for the purpose of saving my breath.

VICKEY   You like to see me in nice clothes.

HOBSON   I do. I like to see my daughters nice. That's why I pay Mr Tudsbury, the draper, £10 a year a head to dress you proper. It pleases the eye and it's good for trade. But, I'll tell you, if some women could see themselves as men see them, they'd have a shock, and I'll have words with Tudsbury an' all, for letting you dress up like guys. I saw you and Alice out of the 'Moonraker's' parlour on Thursday night and my friend Sam Minns –

ALICE   A publican.

HOBSON   Aye, a publican. As honest a man as God Almighty ever set behind a bar, my ladies. My friend, Sam Minns, asked me who you were. And well he might. You were going down Chapel Street with a hump added to nature behind you.

VICKEY   (*scandalized*): Father!

HOBSON   The hump was wagging, and you put your feet on pavement as if you'd got chilblains – aye, stiff neck above and weak knees below. It's immodest!

ALICE   It is not immodest, father. It's the fashion to wear bustles.

HOBSON   Then to hell with the fashion.

MAGGIE   Father, you are not in the 'Moonraker's' now.

VICKEY   You should open your eyes to what other ladies wear. (*Rises*).

HOBSON   If what I saw on you is any guide, I should do nowt of kind. I'm a decent-minded man. I'm Hobson. I'm British middle class and proud of it. I stand for common-sense and sincerity. You're affected, which is bad sense and insincerity.

You've overstepped nice dressing and you've tried grand dressing – (VICKEY *sits*) – which is the occupation of fools and such as have no brains. You forget the majesty of trade and the unparalleled virtues of the British Constitution which are all based on the sanity of the middle classes, combined with the diligence of the working-classes. You're losing balance, and you're putting the things which don't matter in front of the things which do, and if you mean to be a factor in the world in Lancashire or a factor in the house of Hobson, you'll become sane.

VICKEY Do you want us to dress like mill girls?

HOBSON No. Nor like French Madams, neither. It's un-English, I say.

ALICE We shall continue to dress fashionably, father.

HOBSON Then I've no choice for you two. Vickey, you I'm talking to, and Alice. You'll become sane if you're going on living here. You'll control this uppishness that's growing on you. And if you don't, you'll get out of this, and exercise your gifts on someone else than me. You don't know when you're well off. But you'll learn it when I'm done with you. I'll choose a pair of husbands for you, my girls. That's what I'll do.

He will choose husbands for them

ALICE Can't we choose husbands for ourselves?

HOBSON I've been telling you for the last five minutes you're not even fit to choose dresses for yourselves.

MAGGIE You're talking a lot to Vickey and Alice, father. Where do I come in?

HOBSON You? (*Turning to her, astonished.*)

MAGGIE If you're dealing husbands round, don't I get one?

HOBSON Well, that's a good one! (*Laughs.*) You with a husband!

MAGGIE Why not?

HOBSON Why not? I thought you'd sense enough to know. But if you want the brutal truth, you're past the marrying age. You're a proper old maid, Maggie, if ever there was one.

MAGGIE	I'm thirty.
HOBSON	(*facing her*): Aye, thirty and shelved. Well, all the women can't get husbands. But you others, now. I've told you. I'll have less uppishness from you or else I'll shove you off my hands on to some other men. You can just choose which way you like. (*He picks up hat and makes for door.*)
MAGGIE	One o'clock dinner, father.
HOBSON	See here, Maggie. I set the hours at this house. It's one o'clock dinner because I say it is, and not because you do.
MAGGIE	Yes, father.
HOBSON	So long as that's clear I'll go. (*He is by door.*) Oh no, I won't. Mrs Hepworth's getting out of her carriage.

He puts hat on counter again. MAGGIE *rises and opens door. Enter* MRS. H, *an old lady with a curt manner and good clothes.*

HOBSON	Good morning, Mrs Hepworth. What a lovely day! (*He places chair for her.*)
MRS. H	(*sitting*): Morning, Hobson. (*She raises her skirt.*) I've come about those boots you sent me home.
HOBSON	(*kneeling and fondling her foot*): Yes, Mrs Hepworth. They look very nice.
MRS. H:	Get up Hobson. (*He scrambles up, controlling his feelings.*) You look ridiculous on the floor. Who made these boots?
HOBSON	We did. Our own make.
MRS. H	Will you answer a plain question? Who made these boots?
HOBSON	They were made on the premises.
MRS. H	(*to Maggie*): Young woman, you seemed to have some sense when you served me. Can you answer me?
MAGGIE	I think so, but I'll make sure for you, Mrs Hepworth. (*She opens trap and calls.*) Tubby!
HOBSON	You wish to see the identical workman, madam?
MRS. H	I said so.
HOBSON	I am responsible for all work turned out here.

MRS. H   I never said you weren't.

TUBBY WADLOW comes up trap. A white-haired little man with thin legs and a paunch, in dingy clothes with no collar and a coloured cotton shirt. He has no coat on.

TUBBY   Yes, Miss Maggie? (*He stands half out of trap, not coming right up.*)

MRS. H   Man, did you make these boots? (*She rises and advances one pace towards him.*)

TUBBY   No, ma'am.

MRS. H   Then who did? Am I to question every soul in the place before I find out?

TUBBY   They're Willie's making, those.

MRS. H   Then tell Willie I want him.

TUBBY   Certainly ma'am. (*He goes down trap and calls*) Willie!

MRS. H   Who's Willie?

HOBSON   Name of Mossop, madam. But if there is anything wrong I assure you I'm capable of making the man suffer for it. I'll –

WILLIE MOSSOP comes up trap. He is a lanky fellow, about thirty, not naturally stupid but stunted mentally by a brutalized childhood. He is a raw material of a charming man, but, at present, it requires a very keen eye to detect his potentialities. His clothes are an even poorer edition of Tubby's. He comes half-way up trap.

MRS. H   Are you Mossop?

WILLIE   Yes, mum.

MRS. H   You made these boots?

WILLIE   (*peering at them*): Yes, I made them last week.

MRS. H   Take that.

WILLIE, bending down, rather expects 'that' to be a blow. Then he raises his head and finds she is holding out a visiting card. He takes it.

MRS. H   See what's on it?

WILLIE   (*bending over the card*): Writing?

MRS. H   Read it.

WILLIE	I'm trying. (*His lips move as he tries to spell it out.*)
MRS. H	Bless the man. Can't you read?
WILLIE	I do a bit. Only it's such a funny print.
MRS. H	It's the usual italics of a visiting card, my man. Now listen to me. I heard about this shop, and what I heard brought me here for these boots. I'm particular about what I put on my feet.
HOBSON	I assure you it shall not occur again, Mrs Hepworth.
MRS. H	What shan't?
HOBSON	(*crestfallen*): I – I don't know.
MRS. H	Then hold your tongue. Mossop, I've tried every shop in Manchester, and these are the best-made pair of boots I've ever had. Now, you'll make my boots in future. You hear that, Hobson?
HOBSON	Yes, madam, of course he shall.
MRS. H	You'll keep that card, Mossop, and you won't dare leave here to go to another shop without letting me know where you are.
HOBSON	Oh, he won't make a change.
MRS. H	How do you know? The man's a treasure, and I expect you underpay him.
HOBSON	That'll do, Willie. You can go.
WILLIE	Yes, sir.

He dives down trap. MAGGIE *closes it.*

MRS. H	He's like a rabbit.
MAGGIE	Can I take your order for another pair of boots, Mrs Hepworth?
MRS. H	Not yet, young woman. But I shall send my daughters here. And, mind you, that man's to make the boots.
MAGGIE	Certainly, Mrs Hepworth.

HOBSON *opens door.*

MRS. H	Good morning.
HOBSON	Good morning, Mrs Hepworth. Very glad to have the honour of serving you, madam.

She goes out. HOBSON *closes door.*

HOBSON   I wish some people would mind their own business. What does she want to praise a workman to his face for?

MAGGIE   I suppose he deserved it.

HOBSON   Deserved be blowed! Making them uppish. That's what it is. Last time she puts her foot in my shop, I give you my word.

MAGGIE   Don't be silly, father.

HOBSON   I'll show her. Thinks she owns the earth because she lives at Hope Hall.

Enter from street JIM HEELER, *who is a grocer, and Hobson's boon companion.*

JIM   (*looking down street as he enters*): That's a bit of a startler.

HOBSON   (*swinging round*): Eh? Oh, morning, Jim.

JIM   You're doing a good class trade if the carriage folk come to you, Hobson.

HOBSON   What?

JIM   Wasn't that Mrs Hepworth?

HOBSON   Oh yes. Mrs Hepworth's an old and valued customer of mine.

JIM   It's funny you deal with Hope Hall and never mentioned it.

HOBSON   Why, I've made boots for her and all her circle for . . . how long, Maggie? Oh, I dunno.

JIM   You kept it dark. Well aren't you coming round yonder?

HOBSON   (*reaching for his hat*): Yes. That is, no.

JIM   Are you ill?

HOBSON   No. Get away, you girls. I'll look after the shop. I want to talk to Mr Heeler.

JIM   Well, can't you talk in the 'Moonraker's'?

The girls go out to house, MAGGIE *last.*

HOBSON   Yes, with Sam Minns, and Denton and Tudsbury there.

JIM   It's private, then. What's the trouble, Henry?

HOBSON *waves* JIM *into chair and sits.*

HOBSON   They're the trouble. (*Indicates door to house.*) Do your daughters worry you, Jim?

JIM   Nay, they mostly do as I bid them, and the missus does the leathering if they don't. *wife hits daughters*

HOBSON   Ah, Jim, a wife's a handy thing, and you don't know it proper till she's taken from you. I felt grateful for the quiet when my Mary fell on rest, but I can see my mistake now. I used to think I was hard put to it to fend her off when she wanted summat out of me, but the dominion of one woman is Paradise to the dominion of three.

likes the fact that wives dead

JIM   It sounds a sad case, Henry.

HOBSON   I'm a talkative man by nature, Jim. You know that.

JIM   You're an orator, Henry. I doubt John Bright himself is better gifted of the gab than you.

HOBSON   Nay, that's putting it a bit too strong. A good case needs no flattery.

JIM   Well, you're the best debater in the Moonraker's' parlour.

HOBSON   And that's no more than truth. Yes, Jim, in the estimation of my fellow men, I give forth words of weight. In the eyes of my daughters I'm a windbag.

JIM   Nay. Never!

HOBSON   I am. They scorn my wisdom, Jim. They answer back. I'm landed in a hole – a great and undignified hole. My own daughters have got the upper hand of me.

power of women

JIM   Women are worse than men for getting above themselves.

HOBSON   A woman's foolishness begins where man's leaves off.

JIM   They want a firm hand, Henry.

HOBSON   I've lifted up my voice and roared at them.

JIM   Beware at roaring at women, Henry. Roaring is mainly hollow sound. It's like trying to defeat an army with banging drums instead of cold steel. And it's steel in a man's character that subdues the women.

HOBSON   I've tried all ways, and I'm fair moithered. I dunno what to do.

Jim feels the best way to subdue them is to get them married

JIM	Then you quit roaring at 'em and get 'em wed.
HOBSON	I've thought of that. Trouble is to find the men.
JIM	Men's common enough. Are you looking for angels in breeches?
HOBSON	I'd like my daughters to wed temperance young men, Jim.
JIM	You keep your ambitions within reasonable limits, Henry. You've three daughters to find husbands for.
HOBSON	Two, Jim, two.
JIM	Two?

V+A attract costumers
maggie good for business

HOBSON	Vickey and Alice are mostly window dressing in shop. But Maggie's too useful to part with. And she's a bit on the ripe side for marrying, is our Maggie.
JIM	I've seen 'em do it at double her age. Still, leaving her out, you've two.
HOBSON	One'll do for a start, Jim. It's a thing I've noticed about wenches. Get one wedding in a family and it goes through the lot like measles.

First mark maddie and settlement

JIM	Well, you want a man, and you want him temperance. It'll cost you a bit, you know.
HOBSON	Eh? Oh, I'll get my hand down for the wedding all right.
JIM	A warm man like you 'ull have to do more than that. There's things called settlements.
HOBSON	Settlements?
JIM	Aye. You've to bait your hook to catch fish, Henry.
HOBSON	Then I'll none go fishing.

doesn't want to pay for their wedding

JIM	But you said –
HOBSON	I've changed my mind. I'd a fancy for a bit of peace, but there's luxuries a man can buy too dear. Settlements indeed!
JIM	I had a man in mind.
HOBSON	You keep him there, Jim. I'll rub along and chance it. Settlements indeed!
JIM	You save their keep.

HOBSON	They work for that. And they're none of them big eaters.
JIM	And their wages.
HOBSON	Wages? Do you think I pay wages to my own daughters? I'm not a fool.
JIM	Then it's all off?
HOBSON	From the moment that you breathed the word 'settlements' it was dead off, Jim. Let's go to the 'Moonraker's' and forget there's such a thing as women in the world. (*He takes up hat and rings bell on counter.*) Shop! Shop!

MAGGIE *enters.*

HOBSON	I'm going out, Maggie.
MAGGIE	(*she remains by door*): Dinner's at one, remember.
HOBSON	Dinner will be when I come in for it. I'm master here.
MAGGIE	Yes, father. One o'clock.
HOBSON	Come along, Jim.

JIM *and* HOBSON *go out to street.* MAGGIE *turns to speak inside house door.*

MAGGIE	Dinner at half-past one, girls. We'll give him half an hour. (*She closes door and moves to trap, which she raises.*) Willie, come here.

In a moment WILLIE *appears, and stops half-way up.*

WILLIE	Yes, Miss Maggie?
MAGGIE	Come up, and put the trap down; I want to talk to you.

He comes, reluctantly.

WILLIE	We're very busy in the cellar.

MAGGIE *points to trap. He closes it.*

MAGGIE	Show me your hands, Willie.
WILLIE	They're dirty. (*He holds them out hesitatingly.*)
MAGGIE	Yes, they're dirty, but they're clever. They can shape the leather like no other man's that ever came into the shop. Who taught you, Willie? (*She retains his hands.*)
WILLIE	Why, Miss Maggie, I learnt my trade here.

MAGGIE	Hobson's never taught you to make boots the way you do.
WILLIE	I've had no other teacher.
MAGGIE	(*dropping his hands*): And needed none. You're a natural born genius at making boots. It's a pity you're a natural fool at all else.
WILLIE	I'm not much good at owt but leather, and that's a fact.
MAGGIE	When are you going to leave Hobson's?
WILLIE	Leave Hobson's? I – I thought I gave satisfaction.
MAGGIE	Don't you want to leave?
WILLIE	Not me. I've been at Hobson's all my life, and I'm not leaving till I'm made.
MAGGIE	I said you were a fool.
WILLIE	Then I'm a loyal fool.
MAGGIE	Don't you want to get on, Will Mossop? You heard what Mrs Hepworth said. You know the wages you get and you know the wages a bootmaker like you could get in one of the big shops in Manchester.
WILLIE	Nay, I'd be feared to go in them fine places.
MAGGIE	What keeps you here? Is it the – the people?
WILLIE	I dunno what it is. I'm used to being here.
MAGGIE	Do you know what keeps this business on its legs? Two things: one's good boots you make that sell themselves, the other's the bad boots other people make and I sell. We're a pair, Will Mossop.
WILLIE	You're a wonder in the shop, Miss Maggie.
MAGGIE	And you're a marvel in the workshop. Well?
WILLIE	Well, what?
MAGGIE	It seems to me to point one way.
WILLIE	What way is that?
MAGGIE	You're leaving me to do the work, my lad.
WILLIE	I'll be getting back to my stool, Miss Maggie. (*Moves to trap.*)
MAGGIE	(*stopping him*): You'll go back when I've done with

[handwritten annotations in margin: "maggie to be wanting admired" next to the "What keeps you here?" line; "early indication of their partnership" with a circle around the "Two things: one's good boots... We're a pair, Will Mossop" passage]

you. I've watched you for a long time and everything I've
seen, I've liked. I think you'll do for me.

WILLIE What way, Miss Maggie?

MAGGIE Will Mossop, you're my man. Six months I've counted on
you, and it's got to come out some time. *Maggie liked Willia for six months*

WILLIE But I never –

MAGGIE I know you never, or it 'ud not be left to me to do the job
like this.

WILLIE I'll – I'll sit down. (*He sits in arm-chair, mopping his brow.*)
I'm feeling queer-like. What dost want me for?

MAGGIE To invest in. You're a business idea in the shape of a
man. *Maggie wants to start a buisness with Willie*

WILLIE I've got no head for business at all.

MAGGIE But I have. My brain and your hands 'ull make a working
partnership.

WILLIE (*getting up, relieved*): Partnership! Oh, that's a different
thing. I thought you were axing me to wed you.

MAGGIE I am.

WILLIE Well, by gum! And you the master's daughter.

MAGGIE Maybe that's why, Will Mossop. Maybe I've had enough
of father, and you're as different from him as any man I
know.

WILLIE It's a bit awkward-like.

MAGGIE And you don't help me any lad. What's awkward about it?

WILLIE You talking to me like this.

MAGGIE I'll tell you something, Will. It's a poor sort of woman who'll
stay lazy when she sees her best chance slipping from her.
A Salford life's too near the bone to lose things through fear
of speaking out.

WILLIE I'm your best chance?

MAGGIE You are that, Will.

WILLIE Well, by gum! I never thought of this.

MAGGIE Think of it now.

WILLIE I am doing. Only the blow's a bit too sudden to think

very clear. I've a great respect for you, Miss Maggie. You're
a shapely body, and you're a masterpiece at selling in the
shop, but when it comes to marrying, I'm bound to tell you
that I'm none in love with you.

MAGGIE Wait till you're asked. I want your hand in mine and your
word for it that you'll go through life with me for the best
we can get out of it.

WILLIE We'd not get much without there's love between us,
lass.

MAGGIE I've got the love all right.

WILLIE You're desperate set on this. It's a puzzle to me all ways.
What 'ud your father say?

MAGGIE He'll say a lot, and he can say it. It'll make no difference to
me.

WILLIE Much better not upset him. It's not worth while.

MAGGIE I'm judge of that. You're going to wed me, Will.

WILLIE Oh, nay, I'm not. Really I can't do that, Maggie. I can see
that I'm disturbing your arrangements like, but I'll be
obliged if you'll put this notion from you.

MAGGIE When I make arrangements, my lad, they're not made for
upsetting.

WILLIE What makes it so desperate awkward is that I'm
tokened.

MAGGIE You're what? *informs maggie about his former engagment*

WILLIE I'm tokened to Ada Figgins.

MAGGIE Then you'll get loose and quick. Who's Ada Figgins? Do I
know her?

WILLIE I'm the lodger at her mother's.

MAGGIE The scheming hussy. It's not that sandy girl who brings your
dinner?

WILLIE She's golden-haired is Ada. Aye, she'll be here soon.

MAGGIE And so shall I. I'll talk to Ada. I've seen her and I know the
breed. Ada's the helpless sort.

WILLIE   She needs protecting.

MAGGIE   That's how she got you, was it? Yes, I can see her clinging round your neck, until you fancied you were strong. But I'll tell you this, my lad, it's a desperate poor kind of a woman that'll look for protection to the likes of you.

Maggie feels that Ada only wants willie because his strong [handwritten margin note]

WILLIE   Ada does.

MAGGIE   And that gives me the weight of her. She's born to meekness, Ada is. You wed her, and you'll be an eighteen shilling a week bootmaker all the days of your life. You'll be a slave, and a contented slave.

WILLIE   I'm not ambitious that I know of.

MAGGIE   No. But you're going to be. I'll see to that. I've got my work cut out, but there's the makings of a man about you.

WILLIE   I wish you'd leave me alone.

MAGGIE   So does the fly when the spider catches him. You're my man, Willie Mossop.

WILLIE   Aye, so you say. Ada would tell another story, though.

ADA FIGGINS *enters from the street. She is not ridiculous, but a weak, poor-blooded, poor-spirited girl of twenty, in clogs and shawl, with Willie's dinner in a basin carried in a blue handkerchief. She crosses to him and gives him the basin.*

ADA   There's your dinner, Will.

WILLIE   Thank you Ada.

She turns to go, and finds Maggie in her way.

MAGGIE   I want a word with you. You're treading on my foot, young woman.

ADA   Me, Miss Hobson? (*She looks stupidly at Maggie's feet.*)

MAGGIE   What's this with you and him?

ADA   (*gushing*): Oh, Miss 'Obson, it is good of you to take notice like that.

WILLIE   Ada, she –

MAGGIE   You hold your hush. This is for me and her to settle. Take a fair look at him, Ada.

ADA	At Will?
MAGGIE	(*nodding*): Not much for two women to fall out over, is there?
ADA	Maybe he's not so much to look at, but you should hear him play.
MAGGIE	Play? Are you a musician, Will?
WILLIE	I play the Jew's harp.
MAGGIE	That's what you see in him, is it? A gawky fellow that plays the Jew's harp?
ADA	I see the lad I love, Miss 'Obson.
MAGGIE	It's a funny thing, but I can say the same.
ADA	You!
WILLIE	That's what I've been trying to tell you, Ada, and – and, by gum, she'll have me from you if you don't be careful.
MAGGIE	So we're quits so far, Ada.
ADA	You'll pardon me. You've spoke too late. Will and me's tokened.
MAGGIE	That's the past. It's the future that I'm looking to. What's your idea for that?
ADA	You mind your own business, Miss 'Obson. Will Mossop's no concern of thine.
WILLIE	That's what I try to tell her myself, only she will have it it's no use.
MAGGIE	Not an atom. I've asked for your idea of Willie's future. If it's a likelier one than mine, I'll give you best and you can have the lad.
ADA	I'm trusting him to make the future right.
MAGGIE	It's as bad as I thought it was. Willie, you wed me.
ADA	(*weakly*): It's daylight robbery.
WILLIE	Aren't you going to put up a better fight for me than that, Ada? You're fair giving me to her.
MAGGIE	Will Mossop, you take orders from me in this shop. I've told you you'll wed me.
WILLIE	Seems like there's no escape.

ADA   Wait while I get you to home, my lad. I'll set my mother on
        to you.

MAGGIE Oh, so it's her mother made this match?

WILLIE She had above a bit to do with it.

MAGGIE I've got no mother, Will.

WILLIE You need none, neither.

MAGGIE Well, can I sell you a pair of clogs, Miss Figgins?

ADA   No. Nor anything else.

MAGGIE Then you've no business here, have you? (*Moves up to doors
        and opens them.*)

ADA   (*going to him*): Will, are you going to see me ordered out?

WILLIE It's her shop, Ada.

ADA   You mean I'm to go like this?

WILLIE She means it.

ADA   It's cruel hard. (*Moves towards doors.*)

MAGGIE When it comes to a parting, it's best to part sudden and no
        whimpering about it.

ADA   I'm not whimpering, and I'm not parting neither. But he'll be
        whimpering tonight when my mother sets about him.

MAGGIE That'll do.

ADA   Will Mossop, I'm telling you, you'll come home tonight to a
        thick ear. (*She goes.*)

WILLIE I'd really rather wed Ada, Maggie, if it's all same to you.

MAGGIE Why? Because of her mother?

WILLIE She's a terrible rough side to her tongue, has Mrs Figgins.

MAGGIE Are you afraid of her?

WILLIE (*hesitates, then says*): Yes.

MAGGIE You needn't be.

WILLIE Yes, but you don't know her. She'll jaw me till I'm black in
        the face when I go home tonight.

MAGGIE You won't go home tonight.

WILLIE Not go!

MAGGIE You've done with lodging there. You'll go to Tubby

	Wadlow's when you knock off work and Tubby 'ull go round to Mrs Figgins for your things.
WILLIE	And I'm not to go back there never no more?
MAGGIE	No.
WILLIE	It's like an 'appy dream. Eh, Maggie, you do manage things. *He opens the trap.*
MAGGIE	And while Tubby's there you can go round and see about putting the banns up for us two.
WILLIE	Banns! Oh, but I'm hardly used to the idea yet.
MAGGIE	You'll have three weeks to get used to it in. Now you can kiss me, Will.
WILLIE	That's forcing things a bit, and all. It's like saying I agree to everything, a kiss is.
MAGGIE	Yes.
WILLIE	And I don't agree yet. I'm –
MAGGIE	Come along.
	ALICE, *then* VICKEY *enter from house.*
	Do what I tell you, Will.
WILLIE	Now? With them here?
MAGGIE	Yes.
WILLIE	(*pause*): I couldn't. (*He dives for trap, runs down, and closes it.*)
ALICE	What's the matter with Willie?
MAGGIE	He's a bit upset because I've told him he's to marry me. Is dinner cooking nicely?
ALICE	You're going to marry Willie Mossop! Willie Mossop!
VICKEY	You've kept it quiet, Maggie.
MAGGIE	You know about it pretty near as soon as Willie does himself.
VICKEY	Well, I don't know!
ALICE	I know, and if you're afraid to speak your thoughts, I'm not. Look here, Maggie, what you do touches us, and you're mistaken if you think I'll own Willie Mossop for my brother-in-law.

MAGGIE	Is there supposed to be some disgrace in him?
ALICE	You ask father if there's disgrace. And look at me.
	I'd hopes of Albert Prosser till this happened.
MAGGIE	You'll marry Albert Prosser when he's able, and that'll be when he starts spending less on laundry bills and hair cream.

HOBSON *enters from the street.*

HOBSON	Well, what about the dinner?
MAGGIE	It'll be ready in ten minutes.
HOBSON	You said one o'clock.
MAGGIE	Yes, father. One for half-past. If you'll wash your hands it'll be ready as soon as you are.
HOBSON	I won't wash my hands. I don't hold with such finicking ways, and well you know it.
VICKEY	Father, have you heard the news about our Maggie?
HOBSON	News? There is no news. It's the same old tale. Uppishness. You'd keep a starving man from the meat he earns in the sweat of his brow, would you? I'll put you in your places. I'll –
MAGGIE	Don't lose your temper, father. You'll maybe need it soon when Vickey speaks.
HOBSON	What's Vickey been doing?
VICKEY	Nothing. It's about Will Mossop, father.
HOBSON	Will?
ALICE	Yes. What's your opinion of Will?
HOBSON	A decent lad. I've nowt against him that I know of.
ALICE	Would you like him in the family?
HOBSON	Whose family?
VICKEY	Yours.
MAGGIE	I'm going to marry Willie, father. That's what all the fuss is about.
HOBSON	Marry – you – Mossop!
MAGGIE	You thought me past the marrying age. I'm not. That's all.

HOBSON   Didn't you hear me say I'd do the choosing when it came to a question of husbands?

MAGGIE   You said I was too old to get a husband.

HOBSON   You are. You all are.

VICKEY   Father!

HOBSON   And if you're not, it makes no matter. I'll have no husbands here.

ALICE   But you said –

HOBSON   I've changed my mind. I've learnt some things since then. There's a lot too much expected of a father nowadays. There'll be no weddings here.

ALICE   Oh, father!

HOBSON   Go and get my dinner served and talk less. Go on now. I'm not in right temper to be crossed.

He drives Alice and Vickey before him. They go out protesting loudly. But MAGGIE *stands in his way as he follows and she closes the door. She looks at him from the stair.*

MAGGIE   You and I'ull be straight with one another, father. I'm not a fool and you're not a fool, and things may as well be put in their places as left untidy.

HOBSON   I tell you my mind's made up. You can't have Willie Mossop. Why, lass, his father was a workhouse brat. A come-by-chance.

MAGGIE   It's news to me we're snobs in Salford. I'll have Willie Mossop. I've to settle my life's course, and a good course, too, so think on.

HOBSON   I'd be the laughing-stock of the place if I allowed it. I won't have it, Maggie. It's hardly decent at your time of life.

MAGGIE   I'm thirty and I'm marrying Willie Mossop. And now I'll tell you my terms.

HOBSON   You're in a nice position to state terms, my lass.

MAGGIE   You will pay my man, Will Mossop, the same wages as before. And as for me, I've given you the better part of twenty years of work without wages. I'll work eight hours a day in future and you will pay me fifteen shillings by the week.

HOBSON Do you think I'm made of brass?

MAGGIE You'll soon be made of less than you are if you let Willie go. And if Willie goes, I go. That's what you've got to face.

HOBSON I might face it, Maggie. Shop hands are cheap.

MAGGIE Cheap ones are cheap. The sort you'd have to watch all day, and you'd feel happy helping them to tie up parcels and sell laces with Tudsbury and Heeler and Minns supping their ale without you. I'm value to you, so's my man; and you can boast it at the 'Moonraker's' that your daughter Maggie's made the strangest, finest match a woman's made this fifty year. And you can put your hand in your pocket and do what I propose.

HOBSON I'll show you what I propose, Maggie. (*He lifts trap and calls.*) Will Mossop! (*He places hat on counter and unbuckles belt.*) I cannot leather you, my lass. You're female, and exempt, but I can leather him. Come up, Will Mossop.

WILLIE *comes up trap and closes it.*

You've taken up with my Maggie, I hear. (*He conceals strap.*)

WILLIE Nay, I've not. She's done the taking up.

HOBSON Well, Willie, either way, you've fallen on misfortune. Love's led you astray, and I feel bound to put you right. (*Shows strap.*)

WILLIE Maggie, what's this?

MAGGIE I'm watching you, my lad.

HOBSON Mind, Willie, you can keep your job. I don't bear malice, but we must beat the love from your body, and every morning you come here to work with love still sitting in you, you'll get a leathering. (*Getting ready to strike.*)

WILLIE You'll not beat love in me. You're making a great mistake, Mr Hobson, and –

HOBSON You'll put aside your weakness for my Maggie if you've a liking for a sound skin. You'll waste a gradely lot of brass at chemist's if I am at you for a week with this. (*He swings the strap.*)

WILLIE I'm none wanting thy Maggie, it's her that's after me, but I'll tell you this, Mr Hobson: If you touch me with that belt, I'll take her quick, aye, and stick to her like glue.

HOBSON There's nobbut one answer to that kind of talk, my lad. (*He strikes with belt.* MAGGIE *shrinks.*)

WILLIE And I've nobbut one answer back. Maggie, I've none kissed you yet. I shirked before. But, by gum, I'll kiss you now – (*he kisses her quickly, with temper, not with passion, as quickly leaves her, to face Hobson*) – and take you and hold you. And if Mr Hobson raises up that strap again, I'll do more. I'll walk straight out of shop with thee and us two 'ull set up for ourselves.

MAGGIE Willie! I knew you had it in you, lad. (*She puts her arm round his neck. He is quite unresponsive. His hands fall limply to his sides.*)

HOBSON *stands in amazed indecision.*

CURTAIN

ACT TWO

A month later. The shop as Act One. It is about mid-day.
ALICE *is in Maggie's chair at the desk, some ledgers in front of*
her, and VICKEY *is reading behind the counter. The trap is*
open and TUBBY *stands near the desk by Alice.*

ALICE I'm sure I don't know what to tell you to do, Tubby.

TUBBY There's nothing in at all to start on, Miss Alice. We're
worked up.

ALICE Well, father's out and I can't help you.

TUBBY He'll play old Harry if he comes in and finds us doing nowt
in the workroom.

VICKEY Then do something. We're not stopping you.

TUBBY You're not telling me neither. And I'm supposed to take my
orders from the shop.

ALICE I don't know what to tell you. Nobody seems to want any
boots made.

TUBBY The high-class trade has dropped like a stone this last
month. Of course we can go on making clogs for stock if
you like.

ALICE Then you'd better.

TUBBY You know what's got by selling clogs won't pay the rent, let
alone wages, but if clogs are your orders, Miss Alice – (*He
moves towards trap.*)

ALICE You suggested it.

TUBBY I made the remark. (*Starts going down.*) But I'm not a rash
man, and I'm not going to be responsible to the master with
his temper so nowty and all since Miss Maggie went.

ALICE Oh, dear! What would Miss Maggie have told you to do?

TUBBY I couldn't tell you that, Miss, I'm sure. I don't recollect things being as slack as this in her time.

VICKEY You don't help us much for an intelligent foreman.

TUBBY When you've told me what to do, I'll use my intelligence and see it's done properly.

ALICE Then go and make clogs.

TUBBY Them's your orders?

ALICE Yes.

TUBBY Thank you, Miss Alice.

TUBBY *goes down trap and closes it.*

ALICE I wonder if I've done right?

VICKEY That's your look-out.

ALICE I don't care. It's father's place to be here to tell them what to do.

VICKEY Maggie used to manage without him.

ALICE Oh, yes. Go on. Blame me that the place is all at sixes and sevens.

VICKEY I don't blame you. I know as well as you do that it's father's fault. He ought to look after his business himself instead of wasting more time than ever in the 'Moonraker's' but you needn't be snappy with me about it.

ALICE I'm not snappy in myself. (*Sitting at desk.*) It's these figures. I can't get them right. What's 17 and 25?

VICKEY (*promptly*): Fifty-two, of course.

ALICE Well, it doesn't balance right. Oh, I wish I was married and out of it.

VICKEY Same here.

ALICE You!

VICKEY You needn't think you're the only one.

ALICE Well, you're sly, Vickey Hobson. You've kept it to your-self.

VICKEY It's just as well now that I did. Maggie's spoilt our

chances for ever. Nobody's fretting to get Willie Mossop for
a brother-in-law.

MAGGIE *enters, followed by* FREDDIE *and then* WILLIE. *Maggie
and Will are actually about to be married, but their dress
does not specially indicate it. They are not in their older
clothes, and that is all.* FREDDIE *is smarter than either, though
only in his everyday dress. He is not at all a blood, but the
respectable tradesman, and his appearance is such as to
justify his attractiveness in Vickey's eyes.*

ALICE   Maggie, you here!

MAGGIE   I thought we'd just drop in. Vickey, what's this that Mr
               Beenstock's telling me about you and him?

VICKEY   (*sullenly*): If he told you, I suppose you know.

FREDDIE   (*smilingly*): She got it out of me, Vickey.

VICKEY   I don't know that it's any business of yours, Maggie.

MAGGIE   You'll never get no farther with it by yourselves from what I
               hear of father's carryings-on.

VICKEY   That's your fault. Yours and his. (*Indicating* WILLIE *who is
               trying to efface himself at the back.*)

MAGGIE   (*sharply*): Leave that alone. I'm here to help you if you'll
               have my help.

               VICKEY *would say 'No' but* –

FREDDIE   It's very good of you, Miss Maggie, I must say. Your father
               has turned very awkward.

MAGGIE   I reckon he'll change. Has your young man been in yet this
               morning, Alice?

ALICE   (*indignantly*): My young –

MAGGIE   Albert Prosser.

ALICE   No.

MAGGIE   Do you expect him?

ALICE   He's not been here so often since you and Willie Mossop
               got –

MAGGIE   (*sharply*): Since when?

ALICE   Since you made him buy the pair of boots he didn't want.

MAGGIE	I see. He didn't like paying for taking his pleasure in our shop. Well, if he's not expected, somebody must go for him. Prosser, Pilkington & Prosser, Solicitors of Bexley Square. That's right, isn't it?
ALICE	Yes. Albert's 'and Prosser'.
MAGGIE	Aye? Quite a big man in his way. Then, will you go and fetch him, Mr Beenstock? Tell him to bring the paper with him.
VICKEY	(*indignantly*): You're ordering folk about a bit.
MAGGIE	I'm used to it.
FREDDIE	It's all right, Vickey.
ALICE	Is it? Suppose father comes in and finds Albert and Freddy here?
MAGGIE	He won't.
ALICE	He's beyond his time already.
MAGGIE	I know. You must have worried father very badly since I went, Alice.
ALICE	Why?
MAGGIE	Tell them, Mr Beenstock.
FREDDIE	Well, the fact is, Mr Hobson won't come because he's at our place just now.
VICKEY	At your corn warehouse? What's father doing there?
FREDDIE	He's – he's sleeping, Vickey.
ALICE	Sleeping?
FREDDIE	You see, we've a cellar trap in our place that opens in the pavement and your father – wasn't looking very carefully where he was going and he fell into it.
VICKEY	Fell? Is father hurt?
FREDDIE	He's snoring very loudly, but he isn't hurt. He fell soft on some bags.
MAGGIE	Now you can go for Albert Prosser.
ALICE	Is that all we're to be told?
MAGGIE	It's all there is to tell till Freddy's seen his solicitor.
FREDDIE	(*to Vickey*): I'll not be long.
MAGGIE	Don't. I've a job here for you when you get back.

FREDDIE *goes out.*

ALICE   I don't know what you're aiming at, Maggie, but –

MAGGIE   The difference between us is that I do. I always did.

VICKEY   (*indicating Willie*): It's a queer thing you aimed at.

MAGGIE   (*taking Will's arm*): I've done uncommon well myself, and I've come here to put things straight for you. Father told you to get married and you don't shape.

ALICE   He changed his mind.

MAGGIE   I don't allow for folks to change their minds. He made his choice. He said get married, and you're going to.

VICKEY   You haven't made it easier for us, you know.

MAGGIE   Meaning Willie?

WILLIE   It wasn't my fault, Miss Vickey, really it wasn't.

MAGGIE   You call her Vickey, Will.

VICKEY   No, he doesn't.

MAGGIE   He's in the family or going to be. And I'll tell you this. If you want your Freddy, and if you want your Albert, you'll be respectful to my Willie.

ALICE   Willie Mossop was our boot hand.

MAGGIE   He was, and you'll let bygones be bygones. He's as good as you are now, and better.

WILLIE   Nay, come Maggie –

MAGGIE   Better, I say. They're shop assistants. You're your own master, aren't you?

WILLIE   I've got my name wrote up on the windows, but I dunno so much about being master.

MAGGIE   (*producing card*): That's his business card: William Mossop, Practical Boot and Shoe Maker, 39a Oldfield Road, Salford. William Mossop, Master Bootmaker! That's the man you're privileged to call by his Christian name. Aye, and I'll do more for you than let you call him in his name. You can both of you kiss him for your brother-in-law to be.

WILLIE   Nay, Maggie, I'm no great hand at kissing.

VICKEY *and* ALICE *are much annoyed.*

MAGGIE	(*dryly*): I've noticed that. A bit of practice will do you no harm. Come along, Vickey.
ALICE	(interposing): But, Maggie . . . a shop of your own –
MAGGIE	(*grimly*): I'm waiting, Vickey
WILLIE	I don't see that you ought to drive her to it, Maggie.
MAGGIE	You hold your hush.
ALICE	But however did you manage it? Where did the capital come from?
MAGGIE	It came. Will, stand still. She's making up her mind to it.
WILLIE	I'd just as lief not put her to the trouble.
MAGGIE	You'll take your proper place in this family, my lad, trouble or no trouble.
VICKEY	I don't see why you should always get your way.
MAGGIE	It's just a habit. Come along now, Vickey, I've a lot to do today and you're holding everything back.
VICKEY	It's under protest.
MAGGIE	Protest, but kiss.
	VICKEY *kisses* WILL, *who finds he rather likes it. She moves back and starts dusting furiously.*
VICKEY	Your turn now, Alice.
ALICE	I'll do it if you'll help me with these books, Maggie.
MAGGIE	Books? Father's put you in my place?
ALICE	Yes.
MAGGIE	Then he must take the consequences. Your books aren't my affair.
ALICE	I think you might help me, Maggie.
MAGGIE	I'm surprised at you, Alice, I really am, after what you've just been told. Exposing your books to a rival shop. You ought to know better. Will's waiting. And you're to kiss him hearty now.
ALICE	Very well. (*She kisses Will.*)
WILLIE	There's more in kissing nice young women than I thought.
MAGGIE	Don't get too fond of it, my lad.

ALICE   Well, I hope you're satisfied, Maggie. You've got your way again, and now perhaps you'll tell us if there's anything you want in this shop.

MAGGIE   Eh? Are you trying to sell me something?

ALICE   I'm asking you, what's your business here?

MAGGIE   I've told you once. Will and me's taking a day off to put you in the way of getting wed.

VICKEY   It looks like things are slow at your new shop if you can walk round in your best clothes on a working day.

WILLIE   It's not a working day with us. It's a wedding-day.

ALICE   You've been married this morning!

MAGGIE   Not us. I'll have my sisters there when I get wed. It's at one o'clock at St Philip's.

VICKEY   But we can't leave the shop to come.

MAGGIE   Why not? Is trade so brisk?

VICKEY   No, but –

MAGGIE   Not so much high-class trade doing with you, eh?

ALICE   I don't see how you knew.

MAGGIE   I'm good at guessing. You'll not miss owt by coming with us to church, and we'll expect you at home tonight for a wedding-spread.

VICKEY   It's asking us to approve.

MAGGIE   You have approved. You've kissed the bridegroom and you'll go along with us. Father's safe where he is.

ALICE   And the shop?

MAGGIE   Tubby can see the to the shop. And that reminds me. You can sell me something. There are some rings in that drawer there, Vickey.

VICKEY   Brass rings?

MAGGIE   Yes. I want one. That's the size. (*She holds up her wedding-ring finger.*)

VICKEY   That! But you're not taking it for –
         VICKEY *puts box of rings on the counter.*

MAGGIE   Yes, I am. Will and me aren't throwing money round, but we can pay our way. There's fourpence for the ring. Gather it up, Vickey. (*Putting down money and trying on rings.*)

ALICE   Wedded with a brass ring!

MAGGIE   This one will do. It's a nice fit. Alice, you haven't entered that sale in your book. No wonder you're worried with the accounts if that's the way you see to them. (*She puts ring in her bag.*)

ALICE   I'm a bit too much astonished at you to think about accounts. A ring out of stock!

MAGGIE   They're always out of somone's stock.

VICKEY   Well, I'd think shame to myself to be married with a ring like that.

MAGGIE   When folks can't afford the best they have to do without.

VICKEY   I'll take good care I never go without.

MAGGIE   Semi-detached for you, I suppose, and a houseful of new furniture.

ALICE   Haven't you furnished?

MAGGIE   Partly what. We've made a start at the Flat Iron Market.

ALICE   I'd stay single sooner than have other people's cast-off sticks in my house. Where's your pride gone to, Maggie?

MAGGIE   I'm not getting wed myself to help the furnishing trade along. I suppose you'd turn your nose up at second-hand stuff, too, Vickey?

VICKEY   I'd start properly or not at all.

MAGGIE   Then you'll neither of you have any objections to my clearing out the lumber-room upstairs. We've brought a hand-cart round with us.

WILLIE *takes his coat off. He has detachable cuffs which he places carefully on the arm-chair.*

VICKEY   You made sure of things.

MAGGIE   Yes. Get upstairs, Will. I told you what to bring.

ALICE   Wait a bit.

MAGGIE   Go on.

WILLIE *goes into the house.*

ALICE   Let me tell you if you claim the furniture from your old bedroom, that it's my room now, and you'll not budge a stick of it.

MAGGIE   I expected you'd promote yourself, Alice. But I said lumber-room. There's a two-three broken chairs in the attic and a sofa with the springs all gone. You'll not tell me they're of any use to you.

ALICE   Nor to you, neither.

MAGGIE   Will's handy with his fingers. He'll put in this afternoon mending them. They'll be secure against you come to sit on them at supper-time tonight.

VICKEY   And that's the way you're going to live! With cast-off furniture.

MAGGIE   Aye. In two cellars in Oldfield Road.

VICKEY *and* ALICE *A cellar!*

MAGGIE   *Two* of 'em, Alice. One to live and work in and the other to sleep in.

ALICE   Well, it'ud not suit me.

VICKEY   Nor me.

MAGGIE   It suits me fine. And when me and Will are richer than the lot of you together, it'll be a grand satisfaction to look back and think about how we were when we began.

WILLIE *appears with two crippled chairs and begins to cross the shop.*

VICKEY   Just a minute, Will. (*She examines the chairs.*) These chairs are not so bad.

MAGGIE   You can sit on one tonight and see.

VICKEY   You know, mended up, those chairs would do very well for my kitchen when I'm wed.

ALICE   Yes, or for mine.

MAGGIE   I reckon my parlour comes afront of your kitchens, though.

VICKEY   Parlour! I thought you said you'd only one living-room.

MAGGIE   Then it might as well be called a parlour as by any other name. (*Crosses to doors and opens them.*) Put the chairs on the hand-cart, Will.

          WILLIE *goes out to street.*

MAGGIE   And as for your kitchens, you've got none yet, and if you want my plan for you to work, you'll just remember all I'm taking off you is some crippled stuff that isn't yours and what I'm getting for you is marriage portions.

ALICE   What?

VICKEY   Marriage portions, Maggie?

          FREDDIE *re-enters, accompanied by* ALBERT.

MAGGIE   (*To Vickey and Alice*): You'd better put your hats on now, or you'll be late at the church.

VICKEY   But aren't we to know first –?

MAGGIE   (*herding them to exit*): You'll know all right. Be quick with your things now.

          ALICE *and* VICKEY *go out.*

MAGGIE   (*turns*): Good morning, Albert. Have you got what Freddy asked you for?

ALBERT   Yes, but I'm afraid –

          WILLIE *re-enters from street.*

MAGGIE   Never mind being afraid. Freddy, I told you I'd a job here for you. You go upstairs with Will. There's a sofa to come down. Get your coat off to it. Now, then, Albert.

FREDDIE   But –

MAGGIE   I've told you what to do, and you can't do it in your coat. If that sofa isn't here in two minutes, I'll leave the lot of you to tackle this yourselves and a nice hash you'll make of it.

          FREDDIE *takes his coat off.*

FREDDIE   All right, Maggie.

          FREDDIE *goes out.* ALBERT *produces blue paper. She reads.*

MAGGIE   Do you call this English?

ALBERT   Legal English, Miss Hobson.

MAGGIE   I thought it weren't the sort we talk in Lancashire.

What is it when you've got behind the whereases and the saids and to wits?

ALBERT   It's what you told Freddy to instruct me. Action against Henry Horatio Hobson for trespass on the premises of Jonathan Beenstock & Co., Corn Merchants, of Chapel Street, Salford, with damages to certain corn bags caused by falling on them and further damages claimed for spying on the trade secrets of the aforesaid J.B. & Co.

MAGGIE   Well, I'll take your word that this means that – I shouldn't have thought it, but I suppose lawyers are like doctors. They've each a secret language of their own so that if you get a letter from one lawyer you've to take it to another to get it read, just like a doctor sends you to a chemist with a rigmarole that no one else can read, so they can charge you what they like for a drop of coloured water.

ALBERT   I've made this out to your instructions, Miss Hobson, but I'm far from saying it's good law, and I'd not be keen on going into court with it.

MAGGIE   Nobody asked you to. It won't come into court.

WILLIE *and* FREDDIE *enter with a ramshackle horsehair sofa.*

MAGGIE   Open that door for them, Albert.

ALBERT *opens street door. They pass out.*

MAGGIE   What's the time? You can see the clock from there.

ALBERT   (*outside street door*): It's a quarter to one.

MAGGIE   (*flying to living-room door, opening it, and calling*): Girls, if you're late for my wedding I'll never forgive you.

She turns as WILLIE *and* FREDDIE *return.*

MAGGIE   Put your coats on. Now, then, Freddy, you take that paper and put it on *my* father in *your* cellar.

FREDDIE   Now?

MAGGIE   Now? Yes, of course now. He might waken any time.

FREDDIE   He looked fast enough. Aren't I to come to the church?

No one stands to maggie, except Hobson.

demeaning degrading.

MAGGIE	Yes, if you do that quick enough to get there before we're through.
FREDDIE	All right. (*He goes out, pocketing the paper.* MAGGIE *follows him to the door.*)
MAGGIE	Now there's that hand-cart. Are we to take it with us?
ALBERT	To church! You can't do that.
WILLIE	I'll take it home. (*Slight move.*)
MAGGIE	And have me waiting for you at the church? That's not for me, my lad.
ALBERT	You can't very well leave it where it is.
MAGGIE	No. There's only one thing for it. You'll have to take it to our place, Albert.
ALBERT	Me!
MAGGIE	There's the key. (*She hands it from her bag.*) It's 39a, Oldfield Road.
ALBERT	Yes, but to push a hand-cart through Salford in broad daylight!
MAGGIE	It won't dirty your collar.
ALBERT	Suppose some of my friends see me?
MAGGIE	Look here, my lad, if you're too proud to do a job like that, you're not the husband for my sister.
ALBERT	It's the look of the thing. Can't you send somebody from here?
MAGGIE	No. You can think it over. (*She raises trap.*) Tubby!
TUBBY	(*below*): Yes, Miss. (*He appears half-way up trap.*) Why, it's Miss Maggie!
MAGGIE	Come up, Tubby. You're in charge of the shop. We'll all be out for a while.
TUBBY	I'll be up in half a minute, Miss Maggie. (*He goes down and closes trap.*)
MAGGIE	Well, Albert Prosser?
ALBERT	I suppose I must.
MAGGIE	That's right. We'll call it your wedding gift to me, and I'll allow you're putting yourself out a bit for me.

M. Make them do everything for her.

Going with him to the door. He goes. She turns.

Well, Will, you've not had much to say for yourself today. Howst feeling, lad?

WILLIE   I'm going through with it, Maggie.

MAGGIE   Eh?

WILLIE   My mind's made up. I've got wrought up to point. I'm ready.

MAGGIE   It's church we're going to, not the dentist's.

WILLIE   I know. You get rid of summat at dentist's, but it's taking summat on to go to church with a wench, and the Lord knows what.

MAGGIE   Sithee, Will, I've a respect for church. Yon's not the place for lies. The parson's going to ask you will you have me and you'll either answer truthfully or not at all. If you're not willing, just say so now, and –

WILLIE   I'll tell him, 'yes'.

MAGGIE   And truthfully?

WILLIE   Yes, Maggie. I'm resigned. You're growing on me, lass. I'll toe the line with you.

ALICE *and* VICKEY *enter in their Sunday clothes – the same at which Hobson grew indignant in Act One.*

ALICE   We're ready, Maggie.

MAGGIE   And time you were. It's not your weddings that you're dressing for. (*By trap.*) Come up, Tubby, and keep an eye on things.

VICKEY   (*to Will*): Will, have you got the ring?

MAGGIE   I have. do you think I'd trust him to remember?

MAGGIE *goes off with* WILLIE. VICKEY *and* ALICE *are following, laughing.* TUBBY *comes up trap and throws old shoes after them.*

CURTAIN

ACT THREE

*The cellar in Oldfield Road is at once workroom, shop, and
living-room. It is entered from the right corner by a door at
the top of a flight of some seven stairs. Its three windows are
high up at the back – not shop windows, but simply to give
light. Each window has on it 'William Mossop, Practical
Bootmaker', reversed as seen from the inside, and is
illuminated dimly from outside by a neighbouring street
lamp.*

*A door leads to the bedroom. Up stage left is a small screen or
partition whose purpose is to conceal the sink. A shoemaker's
bench, leather and tackle are against the wall, above the
fire-place. Below the door, left, is a small dresser. Table
centre. Seating accommodation consists solely of the sofa
and the two chairs taken from Hobson's, now repaired. The
sofa is left of the table. Crowded on the sofa are, in order,
from down up,* ALBERT, ALICE, VICKEY, FREDDIE.

*As the curtain rises, the four are standing, tea-cups in hand,
saying together: 'The Bride and Bridegroom.' They drink
and sit. General laughter and conversation. On the chair
down stage is* MAGGIE. *From the other chair, centre, behind
table,* WILLIE *rises, nervously, and rushes his little speech
like a child who has learnt a lesson. The table has hot-house
flowers (in a basin) and the remains of a meal at which
tea only has been drunk, and the feast is represented by
the sections of a large pork pie and a small wedding cake.
As* WILL *rises,* ALBERT *hammers on the table.* ALICE *suppresses
him.*

WILLIE It's a very great pleasure to us to see you here tonight.
It's an honour you do us, and I assure you, speaking

for my – my wife, as well as for myself, that the – the –

MAGGIE (*in an undertone*): Generous.

WILLIE Oh, aye. That's it. That the generous warmth of the sentiments so cordially expressed by Mr Beenstock and so enthusiastically seconded by – no, I've gotten that wrong road round – expressed by Mr Prosser and seconded by Mr Beenstock – will never be forgotten by either my life partner or self – and – and I'd like to drink this toast to you in my own house. Our guests, and may they all be married soon themselves.

MAGGIE (*rising and drinking with Will*): Our guests.

WILLIE *and* MAGGIE *sit. General laughter and conversation.*

ALBERT (*solemnly rising*): In rising to respond–

ALICE (*tugging his coat and pulling him into his seat*): Sit down. We've had enough of speeches. I know men fancy themselves when they're talking, but you've had one turn and you needn't start again.

ALBERT But we ought to thank him, Alice.

ALICE I dare say. But you'll not speak as well as he did, so we can leave it with a good wind-up. I'm free to own you took me by surprise, Will.

FREDDIE Very neat speech indeed.

VICKEY Who taught you, Will?

WILLIE I've been learning a lot lately.

ALICE I thought that speech never came natural from Will.

MAGGIE I'm educating him.

FREDDIE Very apt pupil, I must say.

MAGGIE He'll do. Another twenty years and I know which of you three men 'ull be thought most of at the Bank.

FREDDIE That's looking ahead a bit.

MAGGIE I'll admit it needs imagination to see it now.

ALBERT Well, the start's all right, you know. Snug little rooms. Shop of your own. And so on. I was wondering where you raised the capital for this, Maggie.

MAGGIE I? You mustn't call it my shop. It's his.

ALICE   Do you mean to tell me that Willie found the capital?

MAGGIE   He's the saving sort.

ALICE   He must be if you've done this out of what father used to pay him.

MAGGIE   Well, we haven't. Not altogether. We've had help.

ALBERT   Ah!

VICKEY   It's a mystery to me where you got it from.

MAGGIE   Same place as those flowers, Albert.

ALBERT   Hot-house flowers, I see. (*He rises and examines them.*)

MAGGIE   I was wondering where they came from.

         VICKEY *and* FREDDIE *smell flowers.*

MAGGIE   Same place as the money, Albert.

ALBERT   Ah!

ALICE   (*rising*): Well, I think we ought to be getting home, Maggie.

MAGGIE   (*rising, as do the rest*): I shouldn't marvel. I reckon Tubby's a bit tired of looking after the shop by now, and if father's wakened up and come in –

ALICE   That's it. I'm a bit nervous.

MAGGIE   He'll have an edge on his temper. Come and put your hats on.

         She is going with ALICE *and* VICKEY, *then stops.*

MAGGIE   Willie, we'll need this table when they're gone. You'd better be clearing the pots away.

WILLIE   Yes, Maggie.

FREDDIE But – you –

ALBERT   Oh, Lord!

         They laugh.

MAGGIE   (*quite calmly*): And you and Fred can just lend him a hand with the washing-up, Albert.

FREDDIE Me wash pots!

VICKEY   (*really outraged*): Maggie, we're guests.

MAGGIE   I know. Only Albert laughed at Willie, and washing up 'ull maybe make him think on that it's not allowed.

         She ushers ALICE *and* VICKEY *out, and follows.* WILLIE

begins to put pots on tray which he gets from behind screeen.

ALBERT (*after he and Fred have looked at each other, then at Will, then at each other again*): Are you going to wash up pots?

FREDDIE Are you?

ALBERT I look at it like this myself. All being well, you and I are marrying into this family and we know what Maggie is. If we start giving in to her now, she'll be a nuisance to us all our lives.

FREDDIE That's right enough, but there's this plan of hers to get us married. Are you prepared to work it for us?

ALBERT I'm not. Anything but –

FREDDIE Then till she's done it we're to keep the sweet side of Maggie.

ALBERT But, washing pots!

There is a pause. They look at Will, who has brought the tray from behind the screen and is now clearing up the table.

FREDDIE What would you do in our place, Will?

WILLIE Please yourselves. I'm getting on with what she told me.

FREDDIE You're married to her. We aren't.

ALBERT What do you need the table for in such a hurry?

WILLIE Nay, I'm not in any hurry myself.

FREDDIE Maggie wants it for something.

WILLIE It'll be for my lessons, I reckon. She's schooling me.

FREDDIE And don't you want to learn, then?

WILLIE 'Tisn't that. I – just don't want to be rude to you – turning you out so early. I don't see you need to go away so soon.

ALBERT Why not?

WILLIE I'm fond of a bit of company.

ALBERT Do you want company on your wedding night?

WILLIE I don't favour your going so soon.

FREDDIE He's afraid to be alone with her. That's what it is. He's shy of his wife.

They laugh.

WILLIE	That's a fact. I've not been married before, you see. I've not been left alone with her, either. Up to now she's been coming round to where I lodged at Tubby Wadlow's to give me my lessons. It's different now, and I freely own I'm feeling awkward-like. I'd be deeply obliged if you would stay on a bit to help to – to thaw the ice for me.
FREDDIE	You've been engaged to her, haven't you?
WILLIE	Aye, but it weren't for long. And you see, Maggie's not the sort you get familiar with.
FREDDIE	You had quite long enough to thaw the ice. It's not our job to do your melting for you.
ALBERT	No. Fred, these pots need washing. We will wash them.
	ALBERT *carries tray behind screen. Water runs. He is seen flourishing towels.* FREDDIE *is following when* WILLIE *calls him back and takes tray to table.*
WILLIE	Fred, would you like it yourself with – with a wench like Maggie?
FREDDIE	That's not the point. It wasn't me she married.
WILLIE	It's that being alone with her that worries me, and I did think you'd stand by a fellow man to make things not so strange at first.
ALBERT	That's not the way we look at it. Hurry up with those cups, Fred.
	MAGGIE *enters with* VICKEY *and* ALICE *in outdoor clothes.*
MAGGIE	Have you broken anything yet, Albert?
ALBERT	(*indignantly*): Broken? No. (*Takes cup from tray and wipes it.*)
MAGGIE	Too slow to, I expect.
FREDDIE	I must say you don't show much gratitude.
ALBERT	Aren't you all surprised to find us doing this?
MAGGIE	Surprised? I told you to do it.
FREDDIE	Yes, but –
MAGGIE	(*taking towel from him*): You can stop now. I'll finish when you're gone.

Knock at door upstairs.

ALICE   Who's that?

MAGGIE   Someone who can't read, I reckon. You hung that card on
           door, Will?

WILLIE   Aye, it's there. And you wrote it, Maggie.

MAGGIE   I knew better than to trust to you. 'Business suspended for the
           day' it says, and they that can't read it can go on knocking.

HOBSON   (*off, upstairs, after another knock!*): Are you in, Maggie?

VICKEY   (*terrified*): It's father!

ALBERT   Oh, Lord!

MAGGIE   What's the matter? Are you afraid of him?

FREDDIE   Well, I think, all things considered, and seeing –

MAGGIE   All right. We'll consider 'em. You can go into the bedroom,
           the lot of you. . . . No, not you, Willie. The rest. I'll shout
           when I want you.

ALICE   When he's gone.

MAGGIE   It'll be before he's gone.

VICKEY   But we don't want –

MAGGIE   Is this your house or mine?

VICKEY   It's your cellar.

MAGGIE   And I'm in charge of it.

           The four go into bedroom. VICKEY *starts to argue.* ALBERT *opens
           the door.* VICKEY *and* ALICE *go out followed by* FREDDIE *and*
           ALBERT. VICKEY *is pushed inside.* WILL *is going to stairs.*

           You sit you still, and don't forget you're gaffer here. I'll open
           door.

           WILLIE *sits in chair above table.* MAGGIE *goes upstairs and
           opens the door. Enter* HOBSON *to top stair.*

HOBSON   (*with some slight apology*): Well, Maggie.

MAGGIE   (*uninvitingly*): Well, father.

HOBSON   (*without confidence*): I'll come in.

MAGGIE   (*standing in his way*): Well, I don't know. I'll have to ask
           the master about that.

HOBSON   Eh? The master?

MAGGIE   You and him didn't part on the best of terms, you know.
          (*Over the railings.*) Will, it's my father. Is he to come in?

WILLIE   (*loudly and boldly*): Aye, let him come.

          HOBSON *comes downstairs.* MAGGIE *closes door behind him
          and follows.* HOBSON *stares round at the cellar.*

HOBSON   You don't sound cordial about your invitation, young
          man.

WILLIE   Nay, but I am. (*Shaking hands for a long time.*) I'm right
          down glad to see you, Mr Hobson. It makes the wedding-
          day complete-like, you being her father and I – I hope you'll
          see your way to staying a good long while.

HOBSON   Well –

MAGGIE   That's enough, Will. You don't need to overdo it. You can
          sit down for five minutes, father. That sofa 'ull bear your
          weight. It's been tested.

WILLIE   (*taking up teapot*): There's nobbut tea to drink and I reckon
          what's in the pot is stewed, so I'll –

MAGGIE   (*taking pot off him as he moves to fire-place with it*): You'll
          not do owt of sort. Father likes his liquids strong.

WILLIE   A piece of pork pie now, Mr Hobson?

HOBSON   (*groaning*): Pork pie!

MAGGIE   (*sharply*): You'll be sociable now you're here, I hope. (*She
          pours tea at table, top end.*)

HOBSON   It wasn't sociability that brought me, Maggie.

MAGGIE   What was it, then?

HOBSON   Maggie, I'm in disgrace. A sore and sad misfortune's fallen
          on me.

MAGGIE   (*cutting*): Happen a piece of wedding cake 'ull do you
          good.

HOBSON   (*shuddering*): It's sweet.

MAGGIE   That's natural in cake.

          MAGGIE *sits in chair above table.*

HOBSON   I've gotten such a head.

MAGGIE	Aye. But wedding cake's a question of heart. There'd be no bride cakes made at all if we thought first about out heads. I'm quite aware it's foolishness, but I've a wish to see my father sitting at my table eating my wedding cake on my wedding-day.
HOBSON	It's a very serious thing I came about, Maggie.
MAGGIE	It's not more serious than knowing that you wish us well.
HOBSON	Well, Maggie, you know my way. When a thing's done it's done. You've had your way and done what you wanted. I'm none proud of the choice you made and I'll not lie and say I am, but I've shaken your husband's hand, and that's a sign for you. The milk's spilt and I'll not cry.
MAGGIE	(*holding plate*): Then there's your cake, and you can eat it.
HOBSON	I've given you my word there's no ill feeling. (*Pushes cake away.*)
MAGGIE	So now we'll have the deed. (*Pushes it back.*)
HOBSON	You're a hard woman. (*He eats.*) You've no consideration for the weakness of old age.
MAGGIE	Finished?
HOBSON	Pass me that tea.
	She passes: he drinks.
HOBSON	That's easier.
MAGGIE	Now tell me what it is you came about?
HOBSON	I'm in sore trouble, Maggie.
MAGGIE	(*rising and going towards the door*): Then I'll leave you with my husband to talk it over.
HOBSON	Eh?
MAGGIE	You'll not be wanting me. Women are only in your way.
HOBSON	(*rising*): Maggie, you're not going to desert me in the hour of my need, are you?
MAGGIE	Surely to goodness you don't want a woman to help you after all you've said! Will 'ull do his best, I make no

doubt. (*She goes towards the door.*) Give me a call when you've finished, Will.

HOBSON (*following her*): Maggie! It's private.

MAGGIE Why, yes. I'm going and you can discuss it man to man with no fools of women about.

HOBSON I tell you I've come to see you, not him. It's private from him.

MAGGIE Private from Will? Nay, it isn't. Will's in the family and you've nowt to say to me that can't be said to him.

HOBSON I've to tell you this with him there?

MAGGIE Will and me's one.

WILLIE Sit down, Mr Hobson.

MAGGIE You call him father now.

WILLIE (*astonished*): Do I?

HOBSON Does he?

MAGGIE He does. Sit down, Will.

WILLIE *sits right of table.* MAGGIE *stands at the head of the table.* HOBSON *sits on sofa.*

MAGGIE Now, if you're ready, father, we are. What's the matter.

HOBSON That – (*producing the blue paper*) – that's the matter.

MAGGIE *accepts and passes it to Will and goes behind his chair. He is reading upside down. She bends over chair and turns it right way up.*

MAGGIE What is it, Will?

HOBSON (*banging on table*): Ruin, Maggie, that's what it is! Ruin and bankruptcy. Am I vicar's warden at St Philip's or am I not? Am I Hobson of Hobson's Boot Shop on Chapel Street, Salford? Am I a respectable ratepayer and the father of a family or –

MAGGIE (*who has been reading over Will's shoulder*): It's an action for damages for trespass, I see.

HOBSON It's a stab in the back; it's an unfair, un-English, cowardly way of taking a mean advantage of a casual accident.

MAGGIE Did you trespass?

HOBSON   Maggie, I say it solemnly, it is all your fault. I had an accident. I don't deny it. I'd been in the 'Moonraker's' and I'd stayed too long. And why? Why did I stay too long? To try to forget that I'd a thankless child, to erase from the tablets of memory the recollection of your conduct. That was the cause of it. And the result, the blasting, withering result? I fell into that cellar. I slept in that cellar and I awoke to this catastrophe. Lawyers . . . law-costs . . . publicity . . ruin.

MAGGIE   I'm still asking you. Was it an accident? Or did you trespass?

HOBSON   It's an accident. As plain as Salford Town Hall it's an accident, but they that live by law have twisted ways of putting things that make white show as black. I'm in their grip at last. I've kept away from lawyers all my life, I've hated lawyers, and they've got their chance to make me bleed for it. I've dodged them, and they've caught me in the end. They'll squeeze me dry for it.

WILLIE   My word, and that's summat like a squeeze and all.

HOBSON *stares at him.*

MAGGIE   I can see it's serious. I shouldn't wonder if you didn't lose some trade from this.

HOBSON   Wonder! It's a certain as Christmas. My good-class customers are not going to buy their boots from a man who's stood up in open court and had to acknowledge he was overcome at 12 o'clock in the morning. They'll not remember it was private grief that caused it all. They'll only think the worse of me because I couldn't control my daughter better than to let her go and be the cause of sorrow to me in my age. That's what you've done. Brought this on me, you two, between you.

WILLIE   Do you think it will get into the paper, Maggie?

MAGGIE   Yes, for sure. You'll see your name in the *Salford Reporter*, father.

HOBSON   *Salford Reporter!* Yes, and more. When there is ruin and disaster, and outrageous fortune overwhelms a man of my importance to the world, it isn't only the *Salford Reporter* that takes not of it. This awful cross that's come to me will be recorded in the *Manchester Guardian* for the whole of Lancashire to read.

WILLIE   Eh, by gum, think of that! To have your name appearing in the *Guardian!* Why, it's very near worth while to be ruined for the pleasure of reading about yourself in a printed paper.

HOBSON   (*sits sofa*): It's there for others to read besides me, my lad.

WILLIE   Aye, you're right. I didn't think of that. This 'ull give a lot of satisfaction to a many I could name. Other people's troubles is mostly what folks read the paper for, and I reckon it's twice the pleasure to them when it's trouble of a man they know themselves. (*He is perfectly simple and has no malicious intention.*)

HOBSON   To hear you talk it sounds like a pleasure to you.

WILLIE   (*sincerely*): Nay, it's not. You've ate my wedding cake and you've shook my hand. We're friends, I hope, and I were nobbut meditating like a friend. I always think it's best to look on the worst side of things first, then whatever chances can't be worse than you looked for. There's St Philip's now. I don't suppose you'll go on being vicar's warden after this to do, and it brought you a powerful lot of customers from the church, did that.

HOBSON   (*turning to her*): I'm getting a lot of comfort from your husband, Maggie.

MAGGIE   It's about what you deserve.

HOBSON   Have you got any more consolation for me, Will?

WILLIE   (*aggrieved*): I only spoke what came into my mind.

HOBSON   Well, have you spoken it all?

WILLIE   I can keep my mouth shut if you'd rather.

HOBSON   Don't strain yourself, Will Mossop. When a man's

mind is full of thoughts like yours, they're better out than in. You let them come, lad. They'll leave a cleaner place behind.

WILLIE   I'm not much good at talking, and I always seem to say wrong things when I do talk. I'm sorry if my well-meant words don't suit your taste, but I thought you came here for advice.

HOBSON   I didn't come to you, you jumped-up cock-a-hooping – (*Rising.*)

MAGGIE   That'ull do, father. (*Pushes him down.*) My husband's trying to help you.

HOBSON   (*glares impatiently for a time, then meekly says*): Yes, Maggie.

MAGGIE   Now about this accident of yours.

HOBSON   Yes, Maggie.

MAGGIE   It's the publicity that you're afraid of most.

HOBSON   It's being dragged into a court of law at all, me that's voted right all through my life and been a sound supporter of the Queen and Constitution.

MAGGIE   Then we must try to keep it out of court.

HOBSON   If there are lawyers in Heaven, Maggie, which I doubt, they may keep cases out of courts there. On earth a lawyer's job's to squeeze a man and squeeze him where his squirming's seen the most – in court.

MAGGIE   I've heard of cases being settled out of court, in private.

HOBSON   In private? Yes, I dare say, and all the worse for that. It's done amongst themselves in lawyers' offices behind closed doors so no one can see they're squeezing twice as hard in private as they'd dare to do in public. There's some restraint demanded by a public place, but privately! It'll cost a fortune to settle this in private, Maggie.

MAGGIE   I make no doubt it's going to cost you something, but you'd rather do it privately than publicly?

HOBSON   If only it were not a lawyer's office.

MAGGIE	You can settle it with the lawyer out of his office. You can settle with him here.
	She goes and opens door.
MAGGIE	Albert!
	Enter ALBERT, *who leaves door open.*
MAGGIE	This is Mr Prosser, of Prosser, Pilkington, and Prosser.
HOBSON	(*amazed*): He is!
MAGGIE	Yes.
HOBSON	(*incredulously, rising*): You're a lawyer?
ALBERT	Yes, I'm a lawyer.
HOBSON	(*with disgust almost too deep for words*): At your age!
MAGGIE	(*going up to door*): Come out, all of you.
	There is reluctance inside, then VICKEY, ALICE *and* FREDDIE *enter and stand in a row.*
HOBSON	Alice! Vickey!
MAGGIE	Family gathering. This is Mr Beenstock, of Beenstock & Co.
FREDDIE	How do you do?
HOBSON	What! Here!
	The situation is plainly beyond his mused brain's capacity.
MAGGIE	When you've got a thing to settle, you need all the parties to be present.
HOBSON	But there are so many of them. Where have they all come from?
MAGGIE	My bedroom.
HOBSON	Your–? Maggie, I wish you'd explain before my brain gives way.
MAGGIE	It's quite simple. I got them here because I expected you.
HOBSON	You expected me?
MAGGIE	Yes. You're in trouble.
HOBSON	(*shaking his head, then as if finding an outlet, pouncing on Alice*): What's it go to do with Alice and Vickey? What are they doing here? What's happening to the shop?
ALICE	Tubby Wadlow's looking after it.

HOBSON And is it Tubby's job to look after the shop?

VICKEY He'd got no other job. The shop's so slack since Maggie left.

HOBSON (*swelling with rage*): And do you run that shop? Do you give orders there? Do you decide when you can put your hats on and walk out of it?

MAGGIE They come out because it's my wedding-day, father. It's reason enough, and Will and me'ull do the same for them. We'll close the shop and welcome on their wedding-days.

HOBSON Their wedding-days! That's a long time off. It'll be many a year before there's another wedding in this family, I give you my word. (*Turns to Maggie.*) One daughter defying me is quite enough.

ALBERT Hadn't we better get to business, sir?

HOBSON (*turning on him*): Young man, don't abuse a noble word. You're a lawyer. By your own admission you're a lawyer. Honest men live by business and lawyers live by law.

ALBERT In this matter, sir, I am following the instructions of my client, Mr Beenstock, and the remark you have just let fall, before witnesses, appears to me to bear a libellous reflection on the action of my client.

HOBSON What! So it's libel now. Isn't trespass and . . . and spying on trade secrets enough for you, you blood-sucking –

ALBERT One moment, Mr Hobson. You can call me what you like –

HOBSON And I shall. You –

ALBERT But I wish to remind you, in your own interests, that abuse of a lawyer is remembered in the costs. Now, my client tells me he is prepared to settle this matter out of court. Personally, I don't advise him to, because we should probably get higher damages in court. But Mr Beenstock has no desire to be vindictive. He remembers your position, your reputation for respectability, and –

HOBSON   How much?

ALBERT   Er – I beg your pardon?

HOBSON   I'm not so fond of the sound of your voice as you are. What's the figure?

ALBERT   The sum we propose, which will include my ordinary costs, but not any additional costs incurred by your use of defamatory language to me, is one thousand pounds.

HOBSON   What!

MAGGIE   It isn't.

HOBSON   One thousand pounds for tumbling down a cellar! Why, I might have broken my leg.

ALBERT   That is in the nature of an admission, Mr Hobson. Our flour bags saved your legs from fracture and I am therefore inclined to add to the sum I have stated a reasonable estimate of the doctor's bill we have saved you by protecting your legs with our bags.

MAGGIE   Eh, Albert Prosser, I can see you're going to get on in the world, but you needn't be greedy here. That one thousand's too much.

ALBERT   We thought –

MAGGIE   Then you can think again.

FREDDIE   But –

MAGGIE   If there are any more signs of greediness from you two, there'll be a counter-action for personal damages due to your criminal carelessness in leaving your cellar flap open.

HOBSON   Maggie, you've saved me. I'll bring that action. I'll show them up.

MAGGIE   You're not damaged, and one lawyer's quite enough. But he'll be more reasonable now. I know perfectly well what father can afford to pay, and it's not a thousand pounds nor anything like a thousand pounds.

HOBSON   Not so much of your can't afford, Maggie. You'll make me out a pauper.

MAGGIE   You can afford five hundred pounds and you're going to pay five hundred pounds.

HOBSON Oh, but . . . there's a difference between affording and paying.

MAGGIE You can go to the courts and be reported in the papers if you like.

HOBSON It's the principle I care about. I'm being beaten by a lawyer.

VICKEY Father, dear, how can you be beaten when they wanted a thousand pounds and you're only going to give five hundred pounds?

HOBSON I hadn't thought of that.

VICKEY It's they who are beaten.

HOBSON I'd take a good few beatings myself at the price, Vickey. Still, I want this keeping out of court.

ALBERT Then we can take it as settled?

HOBSON Do you want to see the money before you believe me? Is that your nasty lawyer's way?

ALBERT Not at all, Mr Hobson. Your word is as good as your bond.

VICKEY It's settled! It's settled! Hurrah! Hurrah!

HOBSON Well, I don't see what you have to cheer about, Vickey. I'm not to be dragged to public scorn, but you know this is a tidy bit of money to be going out of the family.

MAGGIE It's not going out of the family, father.

HOBSON I don't see how you make it out.

MAGGIE Their wedding-day is not so far off as you thought, now there's a half of five hundred pounds apiece for them to make a start on.

ALBERT *and* ALICE, FREDDIE *and* VICKEY *stand arm in arm.*

HOBSON You mean to tell me –

MAGGIE You won't forget you've passed your word, will you, father?

HOBSON (*rising*): I've been diddled. It's a plant. It –

MAGGIE It takes two daughters off your hands at once, and clears your shop of all the fools of women that used to lumber up the place.

ALICE   It will be much easier for you without us in your way, father.

HOBSON   Aye, and you can keep out of my way and all. Do you hear that, all of you?

VICKEY   Father . . .!

HOBSON   (*picking up his hat*): I'll run that shop with men and – and I'll show Salford how it should be run. Don't you imagine there'll be room for you when you come home crying and tired of your fine husbands. I'm rid of ye, and it's a lasting riddance, mind. I'll pay this money, that you've robbed me of, and that's the end of it. All of you. You, especially, Maggie. I'm not blind yet, and I can see who 'tis I've got to thank for this. (*He goes to foot of stairs.*)

MAGGIE   Don't be vicious, father.

HOBSON   Will Mossop, I'm sorry for you. (*Over banisters.*) Take you for all in all, you're the best of the bunch. You're a backward lad, but you know your trade and it's an honest one.

HOBSON *is going up the stairs.*

ALICE   So does my Albert know his trade.

HOBSON   (*half-way up stairs*): I'll grant you that. He knows his trade. He's good at robbery. (ALICE *shows great indignation*). And I've to have it on my conscience that my daughter's wed a lawyer and an employer of lawyers.

VICKEY   It didn't worry your conscience to keep us serving in the shop at no wages.

HOBSON   I kept you, didn't I? It's someone else's job to victual you in future. Aye, you may grin, you two, but girls don't live on air. Your penny buns 'ull cost you tuppence now – and more. Wait till the families begin to come. Don't come to me for keep, that's all. (*Going.*)

ALICE   Father!

HOBSON   (*turning*): Aye, you may father me. But that's a

piece of work I've finished with. I've done with fathering, and they're beginning it. They'll know what marrying a woman means before so long. They're putting chains upon themselves and I have thrown the shackles off. I've suffered thirty years and more and I'm a free man from today. Lord, what a thing you're taking on! You poor, poor wretches. You're red-nosed robbers, but you're going to pay for it.

He opens door and exits.

MAGGIE   You'd better arrange to get married quick. Alice and Vickey will have a sweet time with him.

FREDDIE   Can they go home at all.

MAGGIE   Why not?

FREDDIE   After what he said?

MAGGIE   He'll not remember half of it. He's for the 'Moonraker's' now – if there's time. What is the time?

ALBERT   Time we were going, Maggie; you'll be glad to see the back of us. (*He shows Maggie his watch.*)

WILLIE   No. No. I wouldn't dream of asking you to go.

MAGGIE   (*moving up to get hats*): Then I would. It's high time we turned you out. There are your hats.

She gets Albert's and Fred's hats from rack.

MAGGIE   Good night.

ALBERT *and* FREDDIE *go upstairs.*

MAGGIE   Good night, Vickey.

VICKEY   (*with a quick kiss*): Good night, Maggie.

VICKEY *goes upstairs. She and* FREDDIE *go out.*

MAGGIE   Good night, Alice.

ALICE   Good night, Maggie. (*The same quick kiss.*) And thank you.

MAGGIE   Oh, that! (*She goes with her to stairs.*) I'll see you again soon, only don't come round here too much, because Will and me's going to be busy and you'll maybe find enough to do yourselves with getting wed.

ALICE   I dare say. (*Upstairs.*)

The general exit is continuous, punctuated with laughter and merry 'Good nights!'

MAGGIE Send us word when the day is.

ALBERT We'll be glad to see you at the wedding.

MAGGIE We'll come to that. You'll be too grand for us afterwards.

ALBERT Oh, no, Maggie.

MAGGIE Well, happen we'll be catching up with you before so long. We're only starting here. Good night.

ALBERT }
ALICE } Good night, Maggie.

They go out, closing door. MAGGIE *turns to* WILL, *putting her hands on his shoulders. He starts.*

MAGGIE Now you've heard what I've said of you tonight. In twenty years you're going to be thought more of than either of your brothers-in-law.

WILLIE I heard you say it, Maggie.

MAGGIE And we're to make it good. I'm not a boaster, Will. And it's to be in less than twenty years, and all.

WILLIE Well, I dunno. They've a long start on us.

MAGGIE And you've got me. Your slate's in the bedroom. Bring it out. I'll have this table clear by the time you come back.

She hustles off the last remains of the meal, putting the flowers on the mantel and takes off cloth, placing it over the back of a chair. WILL *goes to bedroom and returns with a slate and slate pencil. The slate is covered with writing. He puts it on table.*

MAGGIE Off with your Sunday coat now. You don't want to make a mess of that.

He takes coat off and gets rag from behind screen and brings it back to table.

What are you doing with that mopping rag?

WILLIE I was going to wash out what's on the slate.

MAGGIE Let me see it first. That's what you did last night at Tubby's after I came here?

WILLIE   Yes, Maggie.

MAGGIE   (*reading*): 'There is always room at the top.' (*Washing it out.*) Your writing's improving, Will. I'll set you a short copy for tonight, because it's getting late and we've a lot to do in the morning. (*Writing.*) 'Great things grow from small.' Now, then, you can sit down here and copy that.

He takes her place at the table. MAGGIE *watches a moment, then goes to fire-place and fingers the flowers.*

I'll put these flowers of Mrs Hepworth's behind the fire, Will. We'll not want litter in the place come working time tomorrow.

She takes up basin, stops, looks at WILL, *who is bent over his slate, and takes a flower out, throwing the rest behind the fire and going to bedroom with one.*

WILLIE   (*looking up*): You're saving one.

MAGGIE   (*caught in an act of sentiment and apologetically*): I thought I'd press it in my Bible for a keepsake, Will. I'm not beyond liking to be reminded of this day.

She looks at screen and yawns.

MAGGIE   Lord, I'm tired. I reckon I'll leave those pots till morning. It's a slackish way of starting, but I don't get married every day.

WILLIE   (*industrious at his slate*): No.

MAGGIE   I'm for my bed. You finish that copy before you come.

WILLIE   Yes, Maggie.

Exit MAGGIE *to bedroom, with the flower. She closes door,* WILL *copies, repeats letters and words as he writes them slowly, finishes, then rises and rakes out fire. He looks shyly at bedroom door, sits and takes his boots off. He rises, boots in hand, moves towards door, hesitates, and turns back, puts boots down at door, then returns to table and takes off his collar. Then hesitates again, finally makes up his mind, puts out light, and lies down on sofa with occasional glances at the bedroom door. At first he faces the fire. He is uncomfortable. He turns over and faces the door. In a minute* MAGGIE *opens the bedroom door. She has a candle and is in a plain calico night-dress. She comes to* WILL, *shines the light on him, takes him by the ear, and returns with him to bedroom.*

CURTAIN

ACT FOUR

*The scene represents Hobson's living-room, the door to which
was seen in Act One. From inside the room that door is now
seen to be at the left, the opposite wall having the fire-place
and another door to the house.*

It is eight o'clock on a morning a year later.

*In front of the fire-place is a horsehair arm-chair. Chairs to
match are at the table. There are coloured prints of Queen
Victoria and the Prince Consort on the walls on each side of
the door at the back and a plain one of Lord Beaconsfield
over the fire-place. Anti-macassars abound, and the
decoration is quaintly ugly. It is an overcrowded, 'cosy'
room. Hobson is quite contented with it, and doesn't realize
that it is at present very dirty.*

There is probably a kitchen elsewhere, but TUBBY WADLOW *is
cooking bacon at the fire. He is simultaneously laying
breakfast for one on the table. At both proceedings he is a
puzzled and incompetent amateur. Presently the left door
opens, and* JIM HEELER *appears.*

JIM   (*crossing*): I'll go straight up to him, Tubby.

TUBBY   (*checking him*): He's getting up, Mr Heeler.

JIM   Getting up! Why, you said –

TUBBY   I told you what he told me to tell you. Run for Doctor
         MacFarlane, he said. And I ran for Doctor MacFarlane. Now
         go to Mr Heeler, he said, and tell him I'm very ill, and I
         came and told you. Then he said he would get up, and I
         was to have his breakfast ready for him, and he'd see you
         down here.

JIM   Nonsense, Tubby. Of course, I'll go up to him.

TUBBY   You know what he is, sir. I'll get blamed if you go, and he's short-tempered this morning.

JIM   I don't want to get you into trouble, Tubby. (*He sits.*)

TUBBY   Thank you, Mr Heeler.

JIM   I quite thought it was something serious.

TUBBY   If you ask me, it is.

JIM   Which way?

TUBBY   Every way you look at it. Mr Hobson's not his own old self, and the shop's not its own old self, and look at me. Now I ask you, Mr Heeler, man to man, is this work for a foreman shoe hand? Cooking and laying tables and –

JIM   By all accounts there's not much else for you to do.

TUBBY   There's better things than being a housemaid, if it's only making clogs.

JIM   They tell me clogs are a cut line.

TUBBY   Well, what are you do to? There's nothing else wanted. Hobson's in a bad way, and I'm telling no secret when I say it. It's fact that's known.

JIM   It's a thousand pities with an old-established trade like this.

TUBBY   And who's to blame?

JIM   I don't think you ought to discuss that with me, Tubby.

TUBBY   Don't you? I'm an old servant of the master's, and I'm sticking to him now when everybody's calling me a doting fool because I don't look after Tubby Wadlow first, and if that don't give me the right to say what I please, I don't know. It's temper's ruining this shop, Mr Heeler. Temper and obstinacy.

JIM   They say in Chapel Street it's Willie Mossop.

TUBBY   Willie's a good lad, though I say it that trained him. He hit us hard, did Willie, but we'd have got round that in time. With care, you understand, and tact. That's what the gaffer lacks. Miss Maggie, now . . . well, she's a marvel, aye, a fair knock-out. Not slavish, mind you. Stood up to the customers all the time, but she'd a way with her that sold

the goods and made them come again for more. Look at us
now. Men assistants in the shop.

JIM Cost more than women.

TUBBY Cost? They'd be dear at any price. Look here, Mr Heeler,
take yourself. When you go to buy a pair of boots do
you like to be tried on by a man or a nice soft young
woman?

JIM Well –

TUBBY There you are. Stands to reason. It's human nature.

JIM But there are two sides to that, Tubby. Look at the other.

TUBBY Ladies?

JIM Yes.

TUBBY Ladies that are ladies wants trying on by their own sex, and
them that aren't buys clogs. It's the good-class trade that
pays, and Hobson's have lost it.

Enter HOBSON, *unshaven, without collar.*

JIM (*with cheerful sympathy*): Well, Henry!

HOBSON (*with acute melancholy and self-pity*): Oh, Jim! Oh, Jim! Oh,
Jim!

TUBBY Will you sit on the arm-chair by the fire or at the table?

HOBSON The table? Breakfast? Bacon? Bacon, and I'm like this.

JIM *assists him to arm-chair.*

JIM When a man's like this he wants a woman about the house,
Henry.

HOBSON (*sitting*): I'll want then.

TUBBY Shall I go for Miss Maggie, sir? – Mrs Mossop, I mean.

JIM I think your daughters should be here.

HOBSON They should. Only they're not. They're married, and I'm
deserted by them all and I'll die deserted, then perhaps
they'll be sorry for the way they've treated me. Tubby, have
you got no work to do in the shop?

TUBBY I might find some if I looked hard.

HOBSON Then go and look. And take that bacon with you. I don't
like the smell.

TUBBY (*getting bacon*): Are you sure you wouldn't like Miss Maggie here? I'll go for her and – (*He holds the bacon very close to Hobson's face.*)

HOBSON Oh, go for her. Go for the Devil. What does it matter who you go for? I'm a dying man.

TUBBY *takes bacon and goes out.*

JIM What's all this talk about dying, Henry?

HOBSON Oh, Jim! Oh, Jim! I've sent for the doctor. We'll know soon how near the end is.

JIM Well, this is very sudden. You've never been ill in your life.

HOBSON It's been saved up, and all come now at once.

JIM What are your symptoms, Henry?

HOBSON I'm all one symptom, head to foot. I'm frightened of myself, Jim. That's worst. You *would* call me a clean man, Jim?

JIM Clean? Of course I would. Clean in body and mind.

HOBSON I'm dirty now. I haven't washed this morning. Couldn't face the water. The only use I saw for water was to drown myself. The same with shaving. I've thrown my razor through the window. Had to or I'd have cut my throat.

JIM Oh, come, come.

HOBSON It's awful. I'll never trust myself again. I'm going to grow a beard – if I live.

JIM You'll cheat the undertaker, Henry, but I fancy a doctor could improve you. What do you reckon is the cause of it now?

HOBSON 'Moonraker's'.

JIM You don't think–

HOBSON I don't think. I know. I've seen it happen to others, but I never thought that it would come to me.

JIM Nor me, neither. You're not a toper, Henry. I grant you're regular, but you don't exceed. It's a hard thing if a man can't take a drop of ale without it getting back at him like this. Why, it might be my turn next.

TUBBY *enters, showing in* DOCTOR MACFARLANE, *a domineering Scotsman of fifty.*

TUBBY   Here's Doctor MacFarlane.

Exit TUBBY.

DOCTOR   Good morning, gentlemen. Where's my patient?
(*He puts hat on table.*)

JIM   (*speaking without indicating Hobson*): Here. (*He does not rise.*)

DOCTOR   Here? Up?

HOBSON   Looks like it.

DOCTOR   And for a patient who's downstairs I'm made to rise from my bed at this hour?

JIM   It's not so early as all that.

DOCTOR   But I've been up all night, sir. Young woman with her first. Are you Mr Hobson?

JIM   (*quickly*): Certainly not. I'm not ill.

DOCTOR   Hum. Not much to choose between you. You've both got your fate written on your faces.

JIM   Do you mean that I – ?

DOCTOR   I mean he has and you will.

HOBSON   Doctor, will you attend to me?

DOCTOR   Yes. Now, sir. (*He sits by him and holds his wrist.*)

HOBSON   I've never been in a bad way before this morning. Never wanted a doctor in my life.

DOCTOR   You've needed. But you've not sent.

HOBSON   But this morning –

DOCTOR   I ken – well.

HOBSON   What! You know!

DOCTOR   Any fool would ken.

HOBSON   Eh?

DOCTOR   Any fool but one fool and that's yourself.

HOBSON   You're damned polite.

DOCTOR   If ye want flattery, I dare say ye can get it from your friend. I'm giving you ma medical opinion.

HOBSON   I want your opinion on my complaint, not on my character.

DOCTOR Your complaint and your character are the same.

HOBSON Then you'll kindly separate them and you'll tell me –

DOCTOR (*rising and taking up hat*): I'll tell you nothing, sir. I don't diagnose as my patients wish, but as my intellect and sagacity direct. Good morning to you.

JIM But you have not diagnosed.

DOCTOR Sir, If I am to interview a patient in the presence of a third party, the least the third party can do is to keep his mouth shut.

JIM After that, there's only one thing for it. He shifts or I do.

HOBSON You'd better go, Jim.

JIM There are other doctors, Henry.

HOBSON I'll keep this one. I've got to teach him a lesson. Scotchmen can't come over Salford lads this road.

JIM If that's it, I'll leave you.

HOBSON That's it. I can bully as well as a foreigner.

JIM *goes out.*

DOCTOR That's better, Mr Hobson. (*He puts hat down.*)

HOBSON If I'm better, you've not had much to do with it.

DOCTOR I think my calculated rudeness –

HOBSON If you calculate your fees at the same rate as your rudeness, they'll be high.

DOCTOR I calculate by time, Mr Hobson, so we'd better get to business. Will you unbutton your shirt?

HOBSON (*doing it*): No hanky-panky now.

DOCTOR (*ignoring his remark and examining*): Aye. It just confirms ma first opinion, Y've had a breakdown this A.M.?

HOBSON You might say so.

DOCTOR Melancholic? Depressed?

HOBSON (*buttoning shirt*): Question was whether the razor would beat me, or I'd beat razor. I won, that time. The razor's in the yard. But I'll never dare to try shaving myself again.

DOCTOR And do you seriously require me to tell you the cause, Mr Hobson?

HOBSON I'm paying thee brass to tell me.

DOCTOR Chronic alcoholism, if you know what that means.

HOBSON Aye.

DOCTOR A serious case.

HOBSON I know it's serious. What do you think you're here for?
It isn't to tell me something I know already. It's to cure me.

DOCTOR Very well. I will write you a prescription. (*Produces
notebook. Sits at table and writes with copying pencil.*)

HOBSON Stop that!

DOCTOR I beg your pardon.

HOBSON I won't take it. None of your druggist's muck for me. I'm
particular about what I put into my stomach.

DOCTOR Mr Hobson, if you don't mend your manners, I'll certify you
for a lunatic asylum. Are you aware that you've drunk
yourself within six months of the grave? You'd a warning
this morning that any sane man would listen to and you're
going to listen to it, sir.

HOBSON By taking your prescription?

DOCTOR Precisely. You will take this mixture, Mr Hobson, and you
will practise total abstinence for the future.

HOBSON You ask me to give up my reasonable refreshment!

DOCTOR I forbid alcohol absolutely.

HOBSON Much use your forbidding is. I've had my liquor for as
long as I remember, and I'll have it to the end. If I'm to be
beaten by beer I'll die fighting, and I'm none practising
unnatural teetotalism for the sake of lengthening out my
unalcoholic days. Life's got to be worth living before I'll live
it.

DOCTOR (*rising and taking hat again*): If that's the way you talk, my
services are of no use to you.

HOBSON They're not. I'll pay you on the nail for this. (*Rising and
sorting money from pocket.*)

DOCTOR I congratulate you on the impulse, Mr Hobson.

HOBSON Nay, it's a fair deal, doctor. I've had value. You've been a tonic to me. When I got up I never thought to see the 'Moonraker's' again, but I'm ready for my early morning draught this minute. (*Holds out money.*)

DOCTOR (*putting hat down, moving to Hobson and talking earnestly*): Man, will ye no be warned? Ye pig-headed animal, alcohol is poison to ye, deadly, virulent with a system in the state yours is.

HOBSON You're getting warm about it. Will you take your fee? (*Holding out money.*)

DOCTOR Yes. When I've earned it. Put it in your pocket, Mr Hobson. I hae na finished with ye yet.

HOBSON I thought you had.

DOCTOR Do ye ken that ye're defying me? Ye'll die fighting, will ye? Aye, it's a gay, high-sounding sentiment, ma mannie, but ye'll no dae it, do ye hear? Ye'll no slip from me now. I've got ma grip on ye. Ye'll die sober, and ye'll live the longest time ye can before ye die. Have ye a wife, Mr Hobson?

HOBSON *points upward.*

In bed?

HOBSON Higher than that.

DOCTOR It's a pity. A man like you should keep a wife handy.

HOBSON I'm not so partial to women.

DOCTOR Women are a necessity, sir. Have ye no female relative that can manage ye?

HOBSON Manage?

DOCTOR Keep her thumb firm on ye?

HOBSON I've got three daughters, Doctor MacFarlane, and they tried to keep their thumbs on me.

DOCTOR Well? Where are they?

HOBSON Married – and queerly married.

DOCTOR You drove them to it.

HOBSON They all grew uppish. Maggie worst of all.

DOCTOR Maggie? Then I'll tell ye what ye'll do, Mr Hobson.

You will get Maggie back. At any price. At all costs to your
pride, as your medical man I order you to get Maggie back.
I don't know Maggie, but I prescribe her, and – damn ye,
sir, are ye going to defy me again!

HOBSON I tell you I won't have it.

DOCTOR You'll have to have it. You're a dunderheaded lump of
obstinacy, but I've taken a fancy to ye and I decline to let ye
kill yeself.

HOBSON I've escaped from the thraldom of women once, and –

DOCTOR And a pretty mess you've made of your liberty. Now this
Maggie ye mention – if ye'll tell me where she's to be
found, I'll just step round and have a crack with her maself,
for I've gone beyond the sparing of a bit of trouble over
ye.

HOBSON You'll waste your time.

DOCTOR I'll cure you, Mr Hobson.

HOBSON She won't come back.

DOCTOR Oh. Now that's a possibility. If she's a sensible body I
concur with your opinion she'll no come back, but women
are a soft-hearted race and she'll maybe take pity on ye after
all.

HOBSON I want no pity.

DOCTOR If she's the woman that I take her for ye'll get no pity. Ye'll
get discipline.

HOBSON *rises and tries to speak.*

DOCTOR Don't interrupt me, sir. I'm talking.

HOBSON I've noticed it. (*Sits.*)

DOCTOR You asked me for a cure, and Maggie's the name of the cure
you need. Maggie, sir, do you hear? Maggie!

Enter MAGGIE *in outdoor clothes.*

MAGGIE What about me?

DOCTOR (*staggered, then*): Are you Maggie!

MAGGIE I'm Maggie.

DOCTOR Ye'll do.

HOBSON	(*getting his breath*): What are you doing under my roof?
MAGGIE	I've come because I was fetched.
HOBSON	Who fetched you?
MAGGIE	Tubby Wadlow.
HOBSON	(*rising*): Tubby can quit my shop this minute.
DOCTOR	(*putting him back*): Sit down, Mr Hobson.
MAGGIE	He said you're dangerously ill.
DOCTOR	He is. I'm Doctor MacFarlane. Will you come and live here again?
MAGGIE	I'm married.
DOCTOR	I know that, Mrs –
MAGGIE	Mossop.
DOCTOR	Your father's drinking himself to death, Mrs Mossop.
HOBSON	Look here, Doctor, what's passed between you and me isn't for everybody's ears.
DOCTOR	I judge your daughter's not the sort to want the truth wrapped round with a feather-bed for fear it hits her hard.
MAGGIE	(*nodding appreciatively*): Go on. I'd like to hear it all.
HOBSON	Just nasty-minded curiosity.
DOCTOR	I don't agree with you, Mr Hobson. If Mrs Mossop is to sacrifice her own home to come to you, she's every right to know the reason why.
HOBSON	Sacrifice! If you saw her home you'd find another word than that. Two cellars in Oldfield Road.
MAGGIE	I'm waiting, Doctor.
DOCTOR	I've a constitutional objection to seeing patients slip through ma fingers when it's avoidable, Mrs Mossop, and I'll do ma best for your father, but ma medicine willna do him any good without your medicine to back me up. He needs a tight hand on him all the time.
MAGGIE	I've not same chance I had before I married.
DOCTOR	Ye'll have no chance at all unless ye come and live

here. I willna talk about the duty of a daughter because I
doubt he's acted badly by ye, but on the broad grounds of
humanity, it's saving life if ye'll come –

MAGGIE I might.

DOCTOR Nay, but will ye?

MAGGIE You've told me what you think. The rest's my business.

HOBSON That's right, Maggie. (*To Doctor.*) That's what you get
for interfering with folks' private affairs. So now you can
go, with your tail between your legs, Doctor MacFarlane.

DOCTOR On the contrary, I am going, Mr Hobson, with the profound
conviction that I leave you in excellent hands. One
prescription is on the table, Mrs Mossop. The other two are
total abstinence and – you.

MAGGIE (*nodding amiably*): Good morning.

DOCTOR Good morning.

Exit DOCTOR. MAGGIE *picks up prescription and follows to
door.*

MAGGIE Tubby!

She stands by door, TUBBY *just enters inside it.*

MAGGIE Go round to Oldfield Road and ask my husband to come
here and get this made up at Hallow's on your way
back.

TUBBY Yes, Miss – Mrs Mossop.

MAGGIE Tell Mr Mossop that I want him quick.

TUBBY *nods and goes.*

HOBSON Maggie, you know I can't be an abstainer. A man of my
habits. At my time of life.

MAGGIE You can if I come here to make you.

HOBSON Are you coming?

MAGGIE I don't know yet. I haven't asked my husband.

HOBSON You ask Will Mossop! Maggie, I'd better thoughts of you.
Making an excuse like that to me. If you want to come
you'll come so what Will Mossop says, and well you know
it.

MAGGIE   I don't want to come, father. I expect no holiday existence here with you to keep in health. But if Will tells me it's my duty I shall come.

HOBSON   You know as well as I do asking Will's a matter of form.

MAGGIE   Matter of form! My husband a matter of form! He's the –

HOBSON   I dare say, but he is not the man that wears the breeches at your house.

MAGGIE   My husband's my husband, father, so whatever else he is. And my home's my home and all, and what you said of it now to Doctor MacFarlane's a thing you'll pay for. It's no gift to a married woman to come back to the home she's shut of.

HOBSON   Look here, Maggie, you're talking straight and I'll talk straight and all. When I'm set I'm set. You're coming here. I didn't want you when that doctor said it, but, by gum, I want you now. It's been my daughters' hobby crossing me. Now you'll come and look after me.

MAGGIE   All of us?

HOBSON   No. Not all of you. You're eldest.

MAGGIE   There's another man with claims on me.

HOBSON   I'll give him claims. Aren't I your father?

ALICE enters. She is rather elaborately dressed for so early in the day, and languidly haughty.

MAGGIE   And I'm not your only daughter.

ALICE   You been here long, Maggie?

MAGGIE   A while.

ALICE   Ah, well, a fashionable solicitor's wife doesn't rise so early as the wife of a working cobbler. You'd be up when Tubby came.

MAGGIE   A couple of hours earlier.

ALICE   You're looking all right, father. You've quite a colour.

HOBSON   I'm very ill.

MAGGIE	He's not so well, Alice. The doctor says one of us must come and live here to look after him.
ALICE	I live in the Crescent myself.
MAGGIE	I've heard it was that way on. Somebody's home will have to go.
ALICE	I don't think I can be expected to come back to this after what I've been used to lately.
HOBSON	Alice!
ALICE	Well, I say it ought to be Maggie, father. She's the eldest.
HOBSON	And I say you're –

What she is we don't learn, as VICKEY *enters effectively and goes effusively to Hobson.*

VICKEY	Father, you're ill! (*Embracing him.*)
HOBSON	Vickey! My baby! At last I find a daughter who cares for me.
VICKEY	Of course I care. Don't the others? (*Releasing herself from his grasp.*)
HOBSON	You will live with me, Vickey, won't you?
VICKEY	What? (*She stands away from him.*)
MAGGIE	One of us is needed to look after him.
VICKEY	Oh, but it can't be me. In my circumstances, Maggie!
MAGGIE	What circumstances:
ALICE	Don't you know?
MAGGIE	No.

VICKEY *whispers to Maggie.*

HOBSON	What's the matter? What are you all whispering about?
MAGGIE	Father, don't you think you ought to put a collar on before Will comes?
HOBSON	Put a collar on for Will Mossop? There's something wrong with your sense of proportion, my girl.
VICKEY	You're always pretending to folk about your husband, Maggie, but you needn't keep it up with us. We know Will here.

MAGGIE   Father, either I can go home or you can go and put a collar on for Will. I'll have him treated with respect.

ALICE   I expect you'd put a collar on in any case, father.

HOBSON   (*rising*): Of course I should. I'm going to put a collar on. But understand me, Maggie, it's not for the sake of Will Mossop. It's because my neck is cold.

   Exit HOBSON.

MAGGIE   Now, then, which of us is it to be?

VICKEY   It's no use looking at me like that, Maggie. I've told you I'm expecting.

MAGGIE   I don't see that that rules you out. It might happen to any of us.

ALICE   Maggie!

MAGGIE   What's the matter? Children do happen to married women, and we're all married.

ALICE   Well, I'm not going to break my home up and that's flat.

VICKEY   My child comes first with me.

MAGGIE   I see. You've got a house of furniture, and you've got a child coming, so father can drink himself to death for you.

ALICE   That's not fair speaking. I'd come if there were no one else. You know very well it's your duty, Maggie.

VICKEY   Duty? I should think it 'ud be a pleasure to live here after a year or two in cellars.

MAGGIE   I've had thirty years of the pleasure of living with father, thanks.

ALICE   Do you mean to say you won't come?

MAGGIE   It isn't for me to say at all. It's for my husband.

VICKEY   Oh, do stop talking about your husband. If Alice and I don't need to ask our husbands, I'm sure you never need ask yours. Will Mossop hasn't the spirit of a louse and we know it as well as you do.

MAGGIE   Maybe Will's come on since you saw him, Vickey.

It's getting a while ago. There he is now in the shop. I'll go and put it to him.

Exit MAGGIE.

VICKEY   Stop her! (*Going to door.*)

ALICE   (*detaining her*): Let her do it in her own way. I'm not coming back here.

VICKEY   Nor me.

ALICE   There's only Maggie for it.

VICKEY   Yes. But we've got to be careful, Alice. She mustn't have things too much her way.

ALICE   It's our way as well, isn't it?

VICKEY   Not coming is our way. But when she's with him alone and we're not – (*Stopping.*)

ALICE   Yes.

VICKEY   Can't you see what I'm thinking, Alice? It is so difficult to say. Suppose poor father gets worse and they are here, Maggie and Will, and you and I – out of sight and out of mind. Can't you see what I mean?

ALICE   He might leave them his money?

VICKEY   That would be most unfair to us.

ALICE   Father must make his will at once. Albert shall draw it up.

VICKEY   That's it, Alice. And don't let's leave Maggie too long with Will. She's only telling him what to say, and then she'll pretend he thought of it himself. (*She opens door.*) Why, Will, what are you doing up the ladder?

WILLIE   (*off*): I'm looking over the stock.

VICKEY   (*indignantly*): It's father's stock, not yours.

WILLIE   That's so. But if I'm to come into a thing I like to know what I'm coming into.

ALICE   That's never Willie Mossop.

VICKEY   (*still by door*): Are you coming into this?

WILL *enters.* MAGGIE *follows him. He is not aggressive, but he is prosperous and has self-confidence. Against Alice and Vickey he is consciously on his mettle.*

WILLIE	That's the proposal, isn't it?
VICKEY	I didn't know it was.
WILLIE	Now, then, Maggie, go and bring your father down and be sharp. I'm busy at my shop, so what they are at his.
	MAGGIE *takes Will's hat off and puts it on settee, then exits.*
	It's been a good business in its day, too, has Hobson's.
ALICE	What on earth do you mean? It's a good business still.
WILLIE	You try to sell it, and you'd learn. Stock and goodwill 'ud fetch about two hundred.
VICKEY	Don't talk so foolish, Will. Two hundred for a business like father's!
WILLIE	Two hundred as it is. Not as it was in our time, Vickey.
ALICE	Do you mean to tell me father isn't rich?
WILLIE	If you'd not married into the law you'd know what they think of your father today in trading circles. Vickey ought to know. Her husband's in trade!
VICKEY	(*indignantly*): My Fred in trade!
WILLIE	Isn't he?
VICKEY	He's in the wholesale. That's business, not trade. And the value of father's shop is no affair of yours, Will Mossop.
WILLIE	Now I thought maybe it was. If Maggie and me are coming here –
VICKEY	You're coming to look after father.
WILLIE	Maggie can do that with one hand tied behind her back. I'll look after the business.
ALICE	You'll do what's arranged for you.
WILLIE	I'll do the arranging, Alice. If we come here, we come here on my terms.
VICKEY	They'll be fair terms.
WILLIE	I'll see they're fair to me and Maggie.
ALICE	Will Mossop, do you know who you're talking to?
WILLIE	Aye. My wife's young sisters. Times have changed a bit since you used to order me about this shop, haven't they, Alice?

ALICE   Yes, I'm Mrs Albert Prosser now.

WILLIE   So you are, to outsiders. And you'd be surprised the number
         of people that call me Mr Mossop now. We do get on in the
         world, don't we?

VICKEY   Some folks get on too fast.

WILLIE   It's a matter of opinion. I know Maggie and me gave both
         of you a big leg up when we arranged your marriage
         portions, but I dunno that we're grudging you the sudden
         lift you got.

         Enter HOBSON *and* MAGGIE.

WILLIE   Good morning, father. I'm sorry to hear you're not so
         well.

HOBSON   I'm a changed man, Will. (*He comes down and sits on arm-
         chair.*)

WILLIE   There used to be room for improvement.

HOBSON   What! (*He starts up.*)

MAGGIE   Sit down, father.

WILLIE   Aye. Don't let us be too long about this. You've kept me
         waiting now a good while and my time's valuable. I'm busy
         at my shop.

HOBSON   Is your shop more important than my life?

WILLIE   That's a bit like asking if a pound of tea weighs heavier than
         a pound of lead. I'm worried about your life because it
         worrits Maggie, but I'm none worried that bad I'll see my
         business suffer for the sake of you.

HOBSON   This isn't what I've a right to expect from you, Will.

WILLIE   You've no *right* to expect I care whether you sink or
         swim.

MAGGIE   Will.

WILLIE   What's to do? You told me to take a high hand, didn't you?

ALICE   And we're to stay here and watch Maggie and Will abusing
         father when he's ill.

WILLIE   No need for you to stay.

HOBSON   That's a true word, Will Mossop.

VICKEY Father! You take his side against your flesh and blood.

HOBSON That doesn't come too well from you, my girl. Neither of you would leave your homes to come to care for me. You're not for me, so you're against me.

ALICE We're not against you, father. We want to stay and see that Will deals fairly by you.

HOBSON Oh, I'm not capable of looking after myself, amn't I? I've to be protected by you girls lest I'm over-reached, and over-reached by whom? By Willie Mossop! I may be ailing, but I've fight enough left in me for a dozen such as him, and if you're thinking that the manhood's gone from me, you can go and think it somewhere else than in my house.

VICKEY But father – dear father –

HOBSON I'm not so dear to you if you'd think twice about coming here to do for me, let alone jibbing at it the way you did. A proper daughter would have jumped – aye, skipped like a calf by the cedars of Lebanon – at the thought of being helpful to her father.

ALICE Did Maggie skip?

HOBSON She's a bit ancient for skipping exercise, is Maggie; but she's coming round to reconcilement with the thought of living here, and that is more than you are doing, Alice, isn't it? Eh? Are you willing to come?

ALICE (*sullenly*): No.

HOBSON Or you, Vickey?

VICKEY It's my child, father. I –

HOBSON Never mind what it is. Are you coming or not?

VICKEY No.

HOBSON Then you that aren't willing can leave me to talk with them that are.

ALICE Do you mean that we're to go?

HOBSON I understand you've homes to go to.

ALICE Oh, father!

HOBSON Open the door for them, Will.

WILL *rises, crosses, and opens door.* ALICE *and* VICKEY *stare in silent anger. Then* ALICE *sweeps to her gloves on the table.*

ALICE Vickey!

VICKEY Well, I don't know!

MAGGIE (*from her chair by the fire-place*): We'll be glad to see you here at tea-time on a Sunday afternoon if you'll condescend to come sometimes.

VICKEY Beggars on horseback.

VICKEY *and* ALICE *pass out.*

WILL (*closing door*): Nay, come, there's no ill-will. (*He returns to table and sits.*)

HOBSON Now, my lad, I'll tell you what I'll do.

WILLIE Aye, we can come to grips better now there are no fine ladies about.

HOBSON They've got stiff necks with pride, and the difference between you two and them's a thing I ought to mark and that I'm going to mark. There's times for holding back and times for letting loose, and being generous. Now, you're coming here, to this house, both of you, and you can have the back bedroom for your own and the use of this room split along with me. Maggie 'ull keep house, and if she's time to spare she can lend a hand in shop. I'm finding Will a job. You can come back to your old bench in the cellar, Will, and I'll pay you the old wage of eighteen shillings a week and you and me 'ull go equal whacks in the cost of the housekeeping, and if that's not handsome, I dunno what is. I'm finding you a house rent free and paying half the keep of your wife.

WILLIE Come home, Maggie. (*He rises.*)

MAGGIE I think I'll have to. (*She rises.*)

HOBSON Whatever's the hurry for?

WILLIE It may be news to you, but I've a business round in Oldfield Road and I'm neglecting it with wasting my time here.

HOBSON   Wasting time? Maggie, what's the matter with Will? I've made
            him a proposal.

            WILL *is by door.*

MAGGIE   He's a shop of his own to see to, father.

HOBSON   (*incredulous*): A man who's offered a job at Hobson's
            doesn't want to worry with a shop of his own in a wretched
            cellar in Oldfield Road.

WILLIE   Shall I tell him, Maggie, or shall we go?

HOBSON   Go! I don't want to keep a man who – (*Rises.*)

MAGGIE   If he goes, I go with him, father. You'd better speak out,
            Will.

WILLIE   All right, I will. We've been a year in yon wretched
            cellar and do you know what we've done? We've paid
            off Mrs Hepworth what she lent us for our start and made
            a bit o' brass on top o' that. We've got your high-class
            trade away from you. That shop's a cellar, and as you
            say, it's wretched, but they come to us in it, and they
            don't come to you. Your trade's gone down till all you
            sell is clogs. You've got no trade, and me and Maggie's
            got it all and now you're on your bended knees to her
            to come and live with you, and all you think to offer me is
            my old job at eighteen shillings a week. Me that's the
            owner of a business that is starving yours to death.

HOBSON   But – but – you're Will Mossop, you're my old shoe
            hand.

WILLIE   Aye. I were, but I've moved on a bit since then. Your
            daughter married me and set about my education. And –
            and now I'll tell you what I'll do and it'll be the handsome
            thing and all from me to you. I'll close my shop –

HOBSON   Oh! That doesn't sound like doing so well.

WILLIE   I'm doing well, but I'll do better here. I'll transfer to this
            address and what I'll do that's generous is this: I'll take you
            into partnership and give you your half-share on the
            condition you're sleeping partner and you don't try
            interference on with me.

HOBSON A partner! You – here –

WILLIE William Mossop, late Hobson, is the name this shop 'ull have.

MAGGIE Wait a bit, Will. I don't agree to that.

HOBSON Oh, so you have piped up at last. I began to think you'd both lost your senses together.

MAGGIE It had better not be 'late Hobson'.

WILLIE Well, I meant it should.

HOBSON Just wait a bit. I want to know if I'm taking this in aright. I'm to be given a half-share in my own business on condition I take no part in running it. Is that what you said?

WILLIE That's it.

HOBSON Well, I've heard of impudence before, but –

MAGGIE It's all right, father.

HOBSON But did you hear what he said?

MAGGIE Yes. That's settled. Quite settled, father. It's only the name we're arguing about. (*To Will.*) I won't have 'late Hobson's', Will.

HOBSON I'm not dead, yet, my lad, and I'll show you I'm not.

MAGGIE I think Hobson and Mossop is best.

HOBSON His name on my sign-board!

WILLIE The best I'll do is this: Mossop and Hobson.

MAGGIE No.

WILLIE Mossop and Hobson or it's Oldfield Road for us, Maggie.

MAGGIE Very well. Mossop and Hobson.

HOBSON But –

WILLIE (*opening door and looking through*): I'll make some alterations in this shop, and all. I will so. (*He goes through door and returns at once with a battered cane chair.*)

HOBSON Alterations in my shop!

WILLIE In mine. Look at that chair. How can you expect the high-class customers to come and sit on a chair like that? Why, we'd only a cellar, but they did sit on cretonne for their trying on.

HOBSON   Cretonne! It's pampering folk.

WILLIE   Cretonne for a cellar, and morocco for this shop. Folk like to be pampered. Pampering pays. (*He takes the chair out and returns immediately.*) There'll be a carpet on that floor, too.

HOBSON   Carpet! Morocco! Young man, do you think this shop is in Saint Ann's Square, Manchester?

WILLIE   Not yet. But it is going to be.

HOBSON   What does he mean? (*Appealing to heaven.*)

WILLIE   It's no farther from Chapel Street to Saint Ann's Square than it is from Oldfield Road to Chapel Street. I've done one jump in a year and if I wait a bit I'll do the other. Maggie, I reckon your father could do with a bit of fresh air after this. I dare say it's come sudden to him. Suppose you walk with him to Albert Prosser's office and get Albert to draw up the deed of partnership.

HOBSON   (*looking pathetically first at Maggie, then at Willie, rising obediently*): I'll go and get my hat.

   Exit HOBSON.

WILLIE   He's crushed-like, Maggie. I'm afraid I bore on him too hard.

MAGGIE   You needn't be.

WILLIE   I said such things to him, and they sounded as if I meant them, too.

MAGGIE   Didn't you?

WILLIE   Did I? Yes . . . I suppose I did. That's just the worst . . . from me to him. You told me to be strong and use the power that's come to me through you, but he's the old master, and –

MAGGIE   And you're the new.

WILLIE   Master of Hobson's! It's an outrageous big idea. Did I sound confident, Maggie?

MAGGIE   You did all right.

WILLIE   Eh, but I weren't by half so certain as I sounded. Words came from my mouth that made me jump at my own boldness, and when it came to facing you about the name, I tell you I fair trembled in my shoes. I was carried away like, or I'd not have dared to cross you, Maggie.

MAGGIE Don't spoil it, Will. (*Moves to him.*) You're the man I've made you and I'm proud.

WILLIE Thy pride is not in same street, lass, with the pride I have in you. And that reminds me. I've a job to see to.

MAGGIE What job?

WILLIE Oh – about the improvements.

MAGGIE You'll not do owt without consulting me.

WILLIE I'll do this, lass. (*Goes to and takes her hand.*)

MAGGIE What are you doing? You leave my wedding ring alone. (*Wrenches hand free.*)

WILLIE You've worn a brass one long enough.

MAGGIE I'll wear that ring for ever, Will.

WILLIE I was for getting you a proper one, Maggie.

MAGGIE I'm not preventing you. I'll wear your gold for show, but that brass stays where you put it, Will, and if we get too rich and proud we'll just sit down together quiet and take a long look at it, so as we'll not forget the truth about ourselves. . . Eh, lad! (*She touches him affectionately.*)

WILLIE Eh, lass! (*He kisses her.*)

Enter HOBSON *with his hat on.*

MAGGIE Ready, father. Come along to Albert's.

HOBSON (*meekly*): Yes. Maggie.

MAGGIE *and* HOBSON *cross below Will and go out.* WILL *comes down with amazement, triumph and incredulity written on his face, and attempts to express the inexpressible by saying –*

WILLIE Well, by gum! (*He turns to follow the others.*)

CURTAIN

QUESTIONS AND EXPLORATIONS

1 Keeping Track

The questions in this section are designed to help your reading
and understanding of the play in the areas of plot, character,
structure and interaction. They may be used as you read the
play or afterwards, for discussion or for writing. Some are
developed and expanded in the *Explorations* section.

Act One

1 What do we learn about the nature of Hobson's business
   from the opening stage directions?

2 What do we learn about Hobson's character in the opening
   exchange between his daughters?

3 How would Alice react to Albert Prosser?

4 How would Maggie behave as she sells Albert his new
   boots?

5 What do we learn of Maggie's attitude to love and romance?

6 How would Hobson's daughters react when he enters?

7 What impression would Hobson give the audience on his
   first entrance?

8 In what tone would Hobson speak to his daughters about
   their 'uppishness'?

9 How does each of them react to his lecture?

10 How does Hobson treat Mrs Hepworth?

11 What do we learn about Willie Mossop on his first
   appearance?

12 Why does Hobson talk to Jim Heeler in the shop?

13 From this conversation, what do we learn of the conventional relationships between men and women?

14 What attitude would Willie have to Maggie before and after her proposal?

15 How does Maggie react to learning of Willie's engagement?

16 What impression is an audience meant to form of Ada Figgins?

17 Why are Alice and Vickey upset at the news that Maggie intends to marry Willie?

18 How does Hobson react to Maggie's news? How would this reaction be shown?

19 How would an audience react to the climax of Act One?

Act Two

1 How could the passage of time since Act One be shown to an audience?

2 What changes have occurred in the business in the last month?

3 What impression would Maggie and Willie make on their entrance?

4 What accident has befallen Hobson?

5 Why does Maggie force her sisters to kiss Willie?

6 Why does Maggie insist on a brass wedding ring?

7 What is Maggie's plan to help her sisters get married?

8 Why do Freddy and Albert take their orders from Maggie?

9 Has Willie's attitude to Maggie changed? How?

10 Has Maggie's attitude to Willie changed? How?

Act Three

1 What do we learn about Maggie's and Willie's workshop/ home from the stage directions?

2 What is the mood of the wedding party?

3 How does Willie feel about being alone with Maggie? How would this be shown?

4 What is Hobson's attitude to Willie and Maggie on entry?

5 What are Willie's and Maggie's attitudes to Hobson?

6 How would Hobson show his reaction to the 'action for damages'?

7 What is Willie's reaction to Hobson's problem?

8 In making sure that her plan will work, how does Maggie handle her father?

9 How does Hobson's attitude change when his daughters and their suitors appear?

10 How does Hobson react when he realises the plot against him? How would this reaction be shown?

11 How does the atmosphere change after the wedding guests have left?

12 Who provided the money for both the shop and the hothouse flowers?

13 Why does Maggie keep a flower?

14 How would an audience react to the action of the final stage directions?

Act Four

1 What is the atmosphere of Hobson's living-room? How would it be conveyed to the audience?

2 What condition is Hobson now in?

3 Why is Hobson 'frightened of himself'?

4 What is the cause of his condition?

5 What is the tone of his talk with Jim Heeler?

6 What is Dr MacFarlane's attitude to Hobson?

7 What is Hobson's to the doctor?

8 Why is the doctor determined to cure Hobson?

9 How have Alice and Vickey changed in the last year? How would these changes be shown to an audience?

10 What clues are given about the change in Willie Mossop?

11 How has Willie changed? How are these changes shown, both the other characters and to the audience?

12 How do Alice and Vickey leave?

13 Why does Willie reject Hobson's terms?

14 What progress has the Mossops' business made in the last year?

15 What is Hobson's reaction to Willie's offer? How would it be shown?

16 Who now sets the tone for Willie and Maggie's relationship?

17 What is Hobson's final attitude? How would it be shown?

18 Why does Maggie insist on keeping the brass wedding ring?

19 How would Willie show his 'amazement, triumph and incredulity'?

20 How would the audience feel at the end of the play?

2 Explorations

The questions in this section are more detailed and rely on your having read the whole play. Some of the questions develop ideas from the *Keeping Track* section. Because they tend to be more detailed, they offer the opportunity to develop the ideas into written, oral or practical coursework assignments. Some will require a close knowledge of the play; others will require a more imaginative response.

A Characters

Henry Horatio Hobson

1 'I'm a decent-minded man.' What, in Hobson's opinion, makes him decent? Is his self-description appropriate?

2 'There's been a gradual increase of uppishness towards me.' What are the standards of behaviour that Hobson expects from his daughters?

3 'I fell into that cellar. I slept in that cellar and I awoke to this catastrophe.' Outline the reasons for the fall of Hobson throughout the play.

4 'And a pretty mess you've made of your liberty.' Explain the changes that occur in Hobson between Act Three and Act Four.

5 'Your complaint and your character are the same.' What is Hobson's complaint? How does it affect his character?

6 'Hobson's Choice' What eventually is the choice that Hobson faces? How is he finally bought to make this choice.

Maggie Hobson

7 'Courting's like that my lass. All glitter and no use to anybody.' Why might Maggie have come to this opinion about love and marriage?

8 'This is a shop, you know. We're not here to let people go out without buying.' What are the qualities that make Maggie a successful businesswoman?

9 'Where's your pride gone to, Maggie?' Explain the differences in character between Maggie and her sisters.

10 'I don't know what you're aiming at Maggie.' What are the reasons for Maggie organising the plot against her father? Is she justified in doing so?

11 'I don't allow for folks to change their minds.' How does Maggie's single-mindedness affect the other characters in the play?

12 Imagine that Maggie decides to keep a diary from the day that she leaves home. Write her entries for the following days:
i) the day she leaves
ii) her wedding day
iii) six months after her marriage
iv) the day she and Willie return to Hobson's.

Willie Mossop

13 'I'm not ambitious that I know of.' Explain Willie's reactions to:
i) Maggie's proposals.
ii) Hobson's threats in Act One. Why does he change his mind?

14 'Willie! I knew you had it in you, lad.' What indications in Acts One - Three are there of the man Willie will become in Act Four?

15 Imagine that, from their wedding day, Maggie insists on

Willie keeping a diary to help him learn to write. Write
four entries for Willie on:
i) the day after the wedding
ii) the day he and Maggie return to Hobson's.
How will you show the development of his character and
his developing writing skill?

Alice and Vickey Hobson

16 'I'll leave the lot of you to tackle this yourselves and a nice
hash you'll make of it.' What are the characteristics of Alice
and Vickey Hobson? How do they change in the course of
the play?

General

17 Select two of the following: Albert Prosser; Fred Beenstock;
Mrs Hepworth; Tubby Wadlow; Jim Heeler; Ada Figgins;
Dr MacFarlane. How does Brighouse convey their
characters? What are their functions in the play?

18 Create and write a scene that shows a mealtime in the
Hobson household; set it before the play starts (the day
before, for example). Using your understanding of the
characters, show how the meal would be conducted; use
dialogue and stage directions as appropriate. If possible,
include Tubby or Willie.

19 Create and write a scene that shows a mealtime in the
Mossop and Hobson household one month after Maggie
and Willie's return.

20 Select one of the following:
Maggie; Willie; Hobson; Alice and Vickey. Write a
monologue for your selected characters set either:
i) immediately after the end of the play
or
ii) one year later,

which shows the character's attitudes and opinions at that time.
Pay attention to characterisation, vocabulary and expression.
How will you want an audience to react to your character's
speech?

B Themes

1   What, according to Brighouse, are the qualities that make a
    successful business?

2   'Women are worse than men for getting above themselves.'
    What are the accepted conventions between men and
    women as presented in the play?

3   The play is described as a 'Lancashire comedy'. How
    important is the setting of the play?

4   'You ask me to give up my reasonable refreshment.' What
    are the effects of alcohol in the play? What conclusions
    might Brighouse have intended the reader to draw from
    them?

5   Where and when are accepted conventions broken in the
    action of the play? What are the consequences of this?
    What does Brighouse intend the audience to learn?

6   What should an audience learn from the fall of Henry
    Horatio Hobson?

C In Performance

1   Select one of the acts of the play. Using the stage directions
    at the start of the act, draw up a set design brief. What set
    furniture and props would be required? How would you
    dress the set to convey the atmosphere Brighouse intends to
    the audience?

2 Select one of the major characters. What aspects of his/her character would you need as an actor to highlight in performance for the benefit of an audience? How would you use voice/gesture/movement to achieve this?

3 The play is a 'Lancashire comedy'. Select a brief extract and suggest how it might be performed to bring out the comedy intended by the author.

4 Select the character of either Hobson or Willie Mossop. Suggest how an actor playing your chosen character could show the change in the character that occurs in the course of the play.

5 Design a poster advertising a production of the play for your local theatre. Consider how to interest and attract a potential audience, without telling them too much about the play itself.

3 Criticism

1 'The play chronicles a shift in the balance of power between the generations and the sexes.' (Nightingale). Using selected quotations as appropriate, show how this shift occurs in the course of the play.

2 *Hobson's Choice* is a 'play of character rather than of situation'. How far do you agree with this statement?

3 'Brighouse has portrayed these people just as he sees them and the result is true comedy.' Show, using quotations and references as necessary, how the comedy arises from the interplay of the characters.

4 '*Hobson's Choice* will rank among the English plays of the day.' What in your opinion are the qualities which ensured the play's long popularity?

5 'Though local in setting, its intrinsic universality cannot be
   questioned.' (B I Payne). What are the universal qualities
   found in the play?

BIBLIOGRAPHY

Biographical
Harold Brighouse, *What I Have Had* (autobiography), Harrap, 1953

The Theatrical Context
H Hunt, K Richards & J Russell Taylor, *The Revels History of Drama in English: Volume VII 1880 - the present,* Methuen, 1978

Jan McDonald, *The New Drama 1900-1914,* Macmillan, 1986

G Rowell & A Jackson, *The Repertory Movement,* Cambridge, 1984

On *'Hobson's Choice'*
Ben Iden Payne, *A Life in a Wooden O,* Yale, 1977

Criticism
Benedict Nightingale, *An Introduction to 50 Modern British Plays,* Pan, 1982

GLOSSARY

Act One

	axing	asking
	life's too near the bone	life's too hard
17	*tokened*	engaged, betrothed
19	*I'll give you best*	I'll give in to you
20	*she'll jaw me*	she'll lecture me; tell me off
21	*putting the banns up*	posting the announcements of marriage
22	*finicking*	fussy
23	*came-by-chance*	illegitimate
24	*gradely lot of brass*	an awful lot of money
25	*nobbut*	only

Act Two

26	ledgers	account books
	play old Harry	be as angry as the Devil
	nowty	short and changeable
27	*sixes and sevens*	in disorder
28	*a blood*	sharp, aggressive youth
30	*you don't shape*	you've done nothing about it
31	*I'd just as lief*	I'd really rather
32	*wedding spread*	celebratory tea
33	*Flat Iron market*	secondhand furniture/fittings market
34	*parlour*	dining room
35	*marriage portions*	dowries

38	*howst feeling*	how do you feel
	wrought up	worked up
	sithee	now look
	yon's	that's
	throws old shoes	an old custom, to bring good luck to the couple

Act Three

39	*tackle*	equipment and tools
	hothouse	greenhouse
44	*gaffer*	master
46	*sore trouble*	deep, painful trouble
48	*Salford Reporter*	the local newspaper
49	*Manchester Guardian*	the most important local (now national) newspaper
50	*cock-a-hooping*	arrogant; loud-mouthed
51	*mused*	confused
52	*libel*	abuse; defamation, for which one can be sued
53	*defamatory*	damaging to reputation or good name
54	*diddled*	cheated
55	*lumber up*	clutter up
	victual	feed
56	*sweet time*	uncomfortable time
57	*slate*	stone for writing on
59	*calico*	simple cotton

Act Four

60	*anti-macassars*	cloth to protect chairs from hair oil
	Queen Victoria, Prince Albert	Queen and consort in 1881
	Lord Beconsfield	Benjamin Disraeli, Prime Minister
61	*foreman*	leading workman
	cut line	reduced line
63	*toper*	heavy drinker
64	*ken*	know
	ma	my (the doctor's dialogue is written in broad Scots)
65	*sagacity*	wisdom
66	*abstinence/teetotalism*	forgoing all alcoholic drink
68	*dunderheaded*	thickheaded
	thraldom	dominance
	crack	talk
71	*languidly haughty*	lazily superior
74	*mettle*	sharp
76	*worrits*	worries
77	*over-reached*	caught out; fooled
	jibbing	complaining
78	*beggars on horseback*	an insult: 'you think you're so much better than you are!'

79 *sleeping partner*   one who invests in a business but takes no part in running it

80 *cretonne*   a hard-wearing cotton fabric

81 *morocco*   fine goat-skin leather

St Ann's Square   the most exclusive, expensive shopping square of Manchester

Children's Ward

Age 12+

Paul Abbott, John Chambers and Kay Mellor
Granada TV

Six scripts from the popular Granada TV series Children's Ward. The plays trace the fortunes of patients admitted to the children's ward and the relationships between them.

Children's Ward also examines the way the programmes are made, and is an excellent medium for discussing the nature of television drama.

ISBN: 435 23285 1

Whale

David Holman

Whale is based on the real events of October 1988 when three Californian grey whales became trapped under the Arctic ice-cap in Alaska. The play captures the suspense of the rescue and sees the incident through the eyes of both adults and the children who supported the campaign.

  Whale offers many discussion possibilities on green issues, the role of the media and Inuit culture and way of life. The introduction and notes supply ideas, background information and activities for using these opportunities to the full.

ISBN: 435 23286 X

The Crucible

Age 14+

Arthur Miller

The Crucible is a study in the mass hysteria and persecution which led to the 1692 Salem witchcraft trials. It is also a parable for the events of the McCarthy era in the USA of the 1950s. Its sharp analysis of the issues and motivations involved and powerful depictions of people and principles under pressure make this both an incisive and a tragic play.

ISBN: 435 23281 9

The Play of The Monster Garden   Age 10+

Diane Samuels

Based on the popular novel by Vivien Alcock, this tells the
story of Frankie, daughter of the genetic scientist Professor
Stein, and the unexpected results she gets when she
cultivates 'jelly' taken from his laboratory. The resulting tale
is both funny and thoughtful, raising issues surrounding
experimentation, the treatment of living creatures and the
nature of friendship.

ISBN: 435 23284 3
(The novel of *The Monster Garden* is also available in New
Windmills)

The Play of The Secret Diary of Adrian Mole Aged 13¾

Age 13+

Sue Townsend

At nearly 14, Adrian Mole is an intellectual and poet suffering the traumas of first love, parental divorce and spots. And now all this is exposed to the world in a play that retains all the pace, humour and pathos of the original novel. This play will be widely enjoyed both by fans of Adrian Mole and those meeting him for the first time.

ISBN: 435 23283 5

plan looks

Muggie – language is eloquent
and stylish
independent
self-sufficient
admirable

mutual
respect ↓

Willey more colloquial
lack of educated
working class
"father was a work house
bant!

Alice + vicky – self-indulgent
lack of intestin
shop
wemon at worst

↓

altitude p21-22

Act 2 (Pg 26)

Shop. A month later.

Alice + Vicky bad at looking after the Shop.

Maggie and Will's wedding day.

Hobson falls down celler.

Maggies plan

Furniture

Wills declaration of love.

Act 3 (Pg 39)

Will + Maggie's Celler

Wedding, tea, Speeches

Washing up.

Hobson Visits.

Will's ear